AUDACIOUS

The bold, brave, brazen plan to shut down the global child sex industry.*

BY DIANA SCIMONE

* Hint: It's something only you can do.

Peapod Publishing, Inc.

Lake Mary, Florida

Audacious

© 2013 by Diana Scimone

Published by Peapod Publishing, Inc., Lake Mary, Florida U.S.A.

ISBN 978-0-9894591-1-2
Printed in the United States of America
Book cover and design by Cathleen Kwas

www.born2fly.org
www.dianascimone.com
www.peapodpublishing.com

Thank you to my millennial focus group, especially Ryan Brackett and Daniel Shen who read the pre-publication manuscript.

The photo on the front cover is a stock photo; the child in it is not trafficked.

This book belongs to _____

who is an audacious abolitionist with a big idea. If found please return to:

📱 _____

✉️ _____

f _____

t _____

📷 _____

Other: _____

Dedication

This book is dedicated to the unseen little girls in the photo that changed my life. Your horror launched me on this journey. I couldn't rescue you that night but everything I've done since I took that photo, I did for you.

Table of Contents

What's the big idea? Creativity exercises

Trafficked children

Audacious abolitionists

By the numbers

Resources

AUDACIOUS

Day 1

Dear Miss Diana,

I knew you were watching me. I heard the click of your camera as you stood down on the street. I heard the nice man tell you about the cages...how I got here and why they won't let me leave. And I heard you gasp. I didn't do anything wrong. I'm only five years old. Help me. If you can't, please send someone who will.

The girl in the cage

Day 14

Dear Miss Diana,

It's been two weeks since you took the picture. Two weeks since I've been locked here like a prisoner. They've beaten me, starved me, urinated on me, raped me, and abused me. Some of the other girls don't talk anymore. They don't even cry. I'm trying to hold on until you come and get me out of here. They'll keep me here for thirty days and then they say the real horror will begin. If you can't help, send someone who will.

The girl in the cage

Day 29

Dear Miss Diana,

Tomorrow is the thirtieth day. Why didn't you help me? If you couldn't come, why didn't you send someone else? Did you forget about me?

The girl in the cage

This is a fictionalized account of what a child trafficking victim goes through during the grooming process. As horrific as this is, for her the terror is just beginning.

"Ending human trafficking is not idealistic or naive. It is **audacious**. And it is people of **audacity** who change the world."

—Rob Morris, president and co-founder, Love146

The photo that changed my life

o you see the cages in that window?" my contact asked.

"Cages?" I repeated with horror. "What's in them?"

"Five-year-old girls."

I wanted to throw up. With that one sentence my life was about to change. It was early on a Saturday evening in Mumbai, India. I was writing an article about forced prostitution of women, and my contact was taking me through the city's red-light district, which is one of the largest in Asia. As he asked me his question, he pointed to the second floor of a gray, decrepit building.

As a journalist I had been to dozens of countries covering everything from starving refugees in Sudan to people living under the brutal dictatorship in Zimbabwe. I worked at an orphanage for throw-away children in China and interviewed countless Christians who'd been imprisoned and tortured for decades for their faith. I had seen a lot—but never cages that held little girls. My contact went on to tell me that these children are smuggled

"Keep the way of the Lᴏʀᴅ by doing righteousness and justice."

—Genesis 18:19 ɴᴀs

across the border from Nepal into India and held in cages for thirty days. They're raped, tortured, starved, and urinated on until they no longer have a will to rebel or run away. Only then are they fit to be sold as child sex slaves.

"You can take a picture," my contact cautioned, "but don't let the pimps see you or they'll steal your camera."

I got my photo. It's not the best in the world but you can clearly see the bars on the cages. I call it the photo that changed my life. After I got home, I couldn't stop thinking about what I'd seen. I learned there are millions of girls like the ones held in those cages. They're raped for profit thirty or forty times a night—night after night after night. Did I mention there are millions of them? They're not just "over there" but "over here," too. Child trafficking happens not only in third-world countries, but all over the United States in small towns and large cities. With a few clicks of your mouse, you can effortlessly book a child-sex tour—to Atlanta and other cities around the U.S. Pick your child, hair color, sex and age, and she or he will be waiting for you in a hotel room near any major airport. You may think I'm kidding, but I'm not.

Besides sex trafficking, children are also trafficked for labor. All over the world (including in the U.S.) children work illegally in fields, mines, factories, kilns, and on fishing vessels. The cocoa in most of the chocolate you eat is harvested by children. Some of the fish you enjoy is caught by children, whose bodies are thrown overboard at the end of fishing expeditions. Three generations of a family might work in a brick kiln under backbreaking conditions—all to pay off

"Do not follow the crowd in doing wrong. When you give testimony in a lawsuit, do not pervert justice by siding with the crowd."

—Exodus 23:2 NIV

a debt from three generations back. In other areas of the world children are kidnapped and forced to serve as child soldiers; their bodies are pumped with drugs so that they become brutal killing machines. Children are also trafficked for their organs—for their livers, kidneys, lungs, hearts, and eyes. Trafficked children are girls as well as boys.

Child trafficking is organized crime. Human trafficking (adults and children) generates between $30 billion and $34 billion a year—the second-highest grossing illegal industry on the planet after illegal drugs. It's very lucrative with very little risk. You can sell a drug once, but you can sell a person over and over again.

The journey begins

My journey to stop child trafficking began long before that trip to Mumbai. In 1990 I'd just come back from my first trip to China. I was one of the first foreigners allowed in without having to be part of a formal government-run (and controlled) tour—which was a good thing because I was interviewing underground Christians who had spent years in prison for their faith. About a month after I came back from that trip, my mother called me and made a suggestion. "Diana, I've had an idea for a book for you for so long!"

When you're a writer and someone says that to you, you grab the nearest stationary object to hold on to, smile politely, and get prepared to say, "Great idea. Thank you so much. I'll get right on it." My mother wasn't deterred and said, "Being that you like to travel so much, why don't you write a children's book about a little girl and

"A lot of people sell themselves short. They say, 'I'm not the attorney general, so I can't put together an [anti-trafficking] task force in my state.' You can do a lot more than you think."

—Ambassador Luis CdeBaca

"For the Lord your God is…the awesome God who does not show partiality nor take a bribe. He executes justice for the orphan."

—Deuteronomy 10:17-18 NAS

What's the big idea?

Who are you?

What's the big idea? That's what we're going to find out. The big idea is God's audacious plan to end child trafficking that He's going to download to you as you read this book. It's your own, personal, custom-made-just-for-you plan. As you begin to get snippets of this plan, you'll also find out a lot about yourself—because He made you the way you are in order to complete the task He's got for you.

That's the big idea. Throughout this book you'll see "What's the big idea?" pages with some fun things for you to do—they're fun because you'll learn more about yourself and more about God in the process. If you simply read this book without taking the time to do the creativity exercises, you won't get nearly as much out of it; you'll reach the last page and still not really know what God is calling you to do. But I promise you, if you take the time to do these exercises, you'll have a much better idea of who you are and who God created you to be. And how wonderful is that?

Many of the questions I'll be asking you are the ones that my purpose coach, Dr. John Stanko, asked me. John is a board member of Born2Fly and also my brother-in-law. I've heard John teach about purpose for thirty years and his amazing insights have helped me find what God called me to do, and just as importantly given me the oomph to go after my dreams.

There's no particular order to do these "big idea" creativity exercises and you can do them whenever you want. I'm not legalistic about this. You can keep coming back and adding to them—although in this one, don't think too much. Don't let the self-critic answer for you. Just answer quickly and honestly with the first thing that comes to your mind. Your answers don't have to relate to child trafficking or justice; we want to find out about you— who you are and what you love.

What do you like to do? _____

_____

What do you hate doing? _____

What are you good at? _____

_____

What are you not good at? _____

What do your friends always say you're good at? _____

What was your favorite class in school? _____

What was your least fav? _____

What do you wish you would have studied? _____

What would you love to do if money were no object? _____

_____

What would you love to do if you weren't afraid to do it? _____

_____

What would you love to do if your friends, parents, teachers, and Aunt Susie
wouldn't faint if you told them? _____

_____

What do you have absolutely zero interest in doing—even if someone
offered you a million dollars to do? _____

_____

What would you actually pay someone a million dollars to do? _____

_____

As you look over your answers, what pattern do you see? _____

_____

her doll who travel around the world? It would be a great way to introduce kids to other countries and cultures."

It was a brilliant idea. I loved it and wanted to get right on it. There was only one tiny little problem. I was a journalist and had never written a word of fiction or anything creative since, oh, fifth-grade creative writing class. I majored in French, not writing. I loved the idea, however, so I joined a writer's group. I bought books about children's books and read about the different categories of children's lit. I talked with writers, went to meetings, and hung out in the children's section of my local library perched on a little chair reading little books while mothers eyed me suspiciously.

It took me years but I finally had a manuscript. The little girl got dropped from the storyline, and the doll became a dog, who became the main character—PawPaw. I worked with a publishing consultant who told me, "Publishers really like series. If you have faith for one book, can you have faith for three?" Oh, why not. The entire thing was so far beyond my comfort zone that the idea of three books was no more outlandish than one. Suddenly I had a series: *Adventures With PawPaw*. The little white fluffy dog traveled to a different country in each book introducing young children to other countries and cultures—beginning with China, France, and Costa Rica. I dutifully sent the manuscripts to publishers near and far, and it wasn't long before I had the world's largest collection of rejection letters. More than fifty in fact. I wrote to everyone I could think of and had nowhere else to turn, no other options. The project seemed dead in the water—so much time, effort, and money into it with seemingly nothing to show. PawPaw was my pet project yet he

"Do not pervert justice…Follow justice and justice alone, so that you may live and possess the land the Lord your God is giving you."

—Deuteronomy 16:19 NIV

wasn't going anywhere. By this time I had put nearly a decade into the project and it was devastating to me.

One day in between opening rejection letters, I was at lunch reading a World Vision magazine. There was an article about AIDS orphans in Uganda. Keep in mind that this was back in the 1990s when we didn't know what AIDS orphans were. These were kids whose parents had both died of AIDS and rather than break up the family, the oldest child, who might be just ten years old, became the parent and kept the household functioning. The article said there were thousands of these little families all over Uganda.

I don't know what I was eating that day for lunch, but I'm sure it was soaked in tears. They streamed down my face as I read about these kids, picturing a ten year old trying to keep a family together. I was angry and sad and mad all at the same time. "God," I said, "tell me what I can do about this…and don't tell me to send $18 a month to World Vision because You've made me a big-picture person and I want a big-picture answer."

Surprisingly, lightning did not come crashing down around me. In spite of my little hissy fit, God really did answer me. He said one word: PawPaw. Suddenly an idea that wasn't in my head two seconds ago was inside my head—and it takes me longer to tell you than it did to happen. The Lord said, "On the back cover of each one of your books, feature a children's charity in that country. And part of the proceeds from your book sales will go to that charity."

Wow, what a brilliant idea, God! The amazing thing was not just that He answered me, but that He was talking about my books like

7

AUDACIOUS

"Do not deprive the foreigner or the fatherless of justice."

—Deuteronomy 24:17 NIV

Trafficked children

"I don't do windows…oh, wait, I do."

Shyima *does* do windows—and a whole lot more. She cooks, cleans, scrubs, irons, mops, and dusts. She works twenty hours a day, lives in a garage with no light, and doesn't go to school. She never has a day off. Shyima is ten years old. She is a child slave…in California.

Shyima grew up in an impoverished village in Egypt. When her family couldn't pay their debts, they sold her to a wealthy couple who "employed" her as a child maid. The couple moved to California and took Shyima with them. While the family's own children lived in opulence, Shyima lived in a garage with no light. She did all the laundry, cooking, and cleaning for the family—and never went to school. The couple didn't work and she was at their call 24/7. She earned $45 a month.

Why would parents sell their child? Because to them even the dark garage where Shyima slept was better than the impoverished conditions she came from. "Families in remote villages send their daughters to work in cities for extra money and the opportunity to escape a dead-end life," says Rukmini Callimachi, who investigated child slavery for the Associated Press.[*]

Why didn't Shyima run away? It never occurred to her. In fact she thought her situation was normal. Thankfully her California neighbors realized the situation was not normal and called the police. Shyima was rescued, placed in foster care, and finally adopted. The couple who held her captive was arrested on charges of child slavery, imprisoned, and then deported.

Sadly, the wife is once again operating a child labor ring in Egypt from the very apartment where she once held Shyima captive. Sadly, another child has taken Shyima's place—and thousands more will unless we stop this horror. Each year thousands of children are trafficked and forced to work as household slaves. The problem is so well hidden that even the United Nations, Interpol, and U.S. State Department have no idea how many child maids work in the U.S.

---

[*] Child Maid Trafficking Spreads from Africa to US, by Rukmini Callimachi, Associated Press

they were really going to get published. Remember, at that point all I had were three manuscripts and the world's largest collection of rejection letters. I wish I could tell you that in the same pile of mail was an acceptance letter from a publisher, but that's not how it happened. Instead my collection grew and grew until finally one day out of desperation I decided to publish my books myself. I actually started my own publishing company, Peapod Publishing, incorporated it and everything—solely so that I could do my own books. I worked with an illustrator, Leah Wiedemer, who made PawPaw come alive on the pages of his adventures.

This was just when self-publishing was coming into existence, but at that time the self-publisher printing presses in the U.S. couldn't print books in color—only adult books. But they could in China. So I worked with a printer inside China and negotiated everything by email. The day I hired a customs broker was the day I knew my life had officially gotten crazy. What in the world was I doing following my dream to such a ludicrous extent?

Because when you have a dream, you can't let go of it. And it won't let go of you.

One day a truck arrived on my doorstep and the driver and I unloaded seventy-five boxes of *Adventures With PawPaw* books. As we were schlepping them from the truck into every closet where I could find a spot, the driver stopped to look at the pictures on my office wall. I'm a journalist, not a photographer, and usually my photographs are passable, but from way back when there was something about my photos of kids that stood out. It wasn't just

"I fear that we live in a world where people are more in love with the idea of changing the world instead of actually changing the world."

—Eugene Cho

AUDACIOUS

"Cursed is anyone who withholds justice from the foreigner, the fatherless or the widow."

—Deuteronomy 27:19 NIV

Trafficked children

Begging

I can't get a picture out of my head. Recently my anti-trafficking colleague, Pat Bradley, was in town. Pat is president of International Crisis Aid (ICA), which does great work rescuing trafficked kids in Cambodia, Ethiopia, and also in his home state of Missouri in the U.S. He had just returned from Ethiopia where ICA has built some safe houses for the little girls they rescue from forced prostitution. Pat and his colleagues were in the red-light district one night to rescue girls trapped in the horror of child sex trafficking. They could rescue only a certain number of girls because that's all the room they had in their safe houses.

But more girls showed up. A lot of them. And this is the picture I can't get out of my mind: The little girls ran up to Pat carrying all their worldly possessions in little plastic bags—and they begged him to take them away from the horror. And he had to say no. I can't even imagine the pain in his heart at having to do that. I cried for thirty-six hours after he told me.

You might say, "Why didn't he just take them all? Figure out what to do once he had them." Easy to say from your comfortable chair reading this. Where would you take 100 traumatized little girls? You can't just hail a cab. You can't just show up on someone's doorstep and say, "Can you take a girl or two? Feed them, clean them, house them, heal them, love them? Hide them from the pimps who'll try to steal them back?"

Someone once accused me of constantly begging for money for Born2Fly. "Something must be wrong if you're always needing money," this person wrote in an email. "I'm going to ask God what's wrong in your life. There must be sin somewhere that He's not blessing your efforts."

Ooookay. I'm not above begging for money to help little girls like the ones I can't get out of my mind. Forgive me for begging…but if those little girls can do it, so can I.

the kids themselves. It was the photos of the kids themselves.
They were actually really, really good. I can say that without pride
because it was a God thing and I recognized it. In fact, I had sixteen
of these photos framed and hanging on the walls of my office.
That's what the driver was looking at as we unloaded the books.
"You sure have a lot of children," he said smiling in wonder. Another
God thing, I knew, and I filed it away in the back of my mind.

Because I'm a big-picture person, I assumed that when God told
me part of the profits from the books would go to help children, He
meant I would be selling millions of PawPaw books, with millions of
dollars coming in to fund children's charities. So like any big-picture
person, I started a charity to administrate it all, incorporated, got
a board of directors, wrote by-laws, and applied to the IRS for
501c3 non-profit status. Their reply came back in thirty days—
virtually unheard of for anyone applying for non-profit status. (Ask
around; you'll see what I mean.) Suddenly I was president of a
publishing company *and* a children's charity—the non-profit that
would later become Born to Fly International, or The Born2Fly
Project. My friends graciously bought books. My relatives graciously
bought books. Friends of my relatives, and relatives of my friends
bought books. It wasn't long before I learned that writing a book
is the easy part; selling it is the hard part. I would love to tell you
I sold out all the books in a month, and that millions of dollars of
donations came in to the charity, but I'd be lying. We started small—
our first donation was $5, which I sent with my brother-in-law
and board member, Dr. John Stanko, when he went on a medical-
educational team to Afghanistan, asking him to invest it in children

"Today, you
can buy a
human being
for $200 in any
major city in
the world."

—Carmen Pitre

"He is the Rock, His work is perfect; for all His ways are justice, a God of truth and without injustice."

—Deuteronomy 32:4 NKJV

What's the big idea?

Questions about life and other random stuff

One of my Twitter friends, @jnswanson (aka Jon Swanson), came up with "discernment questions" to help people think about jobs, careers, and life. "That's hard for some of us," he explains. "We don't know what we want to be when we grow up. We can't exactly tell you what we've always dreamed of doing. So I sent one of them this worksheet. I tried to move from big, 'I want to change the whole world' kinds of questions to smaller, specific kinds of questions. Forget job categories for a little bit. Think about the things that you like/love to do. Just make a list."

I love helping _____ think more clearly about _____.

I love doing the _____ part of _____

kind of events. I don't like doing the _____ part

of those events. And I don't like _____ events at all.

I like to help _____ (kind of person)

by doing _____.

I love when I'm given _____ and can fill in _____.

I learn best when I can _____.

I love baking cookies because _____

I know that I have mixed motives about _____

but _____ percent of my motive is pure.

I have no idea where I will be in five years, but part of the uncertainty is

because I really want to _____,

but that's not up to me and I would be thrilled if God would let me

_____, but I'm not sure.

The moments at college/current job/volunteering that I have loved most

have been when _____ and

_____ and _____.

I am best as part of a team where I get to _____ and

someone else is _____ and a couple

other people are _____.

* Jon Swanson, 300 Words a Day Following Jesus, Discernment questions, March 5, 2013, http://300wordsaday.com/2013/03/05/discernment-questions/

AUDACIOUS

14

in Afghanistan. (He gave it to a doctor to buy eye ointment for kids.) Our donations grew slowly but surely. When the tsunami hit, we raised nearly $10,000 and gave all of it to charities on the ground in affected countries—charities I knew personally because of my prior work as a journalist.

Meanwhile I was doing everything I could to sell more PawPaw books to fund it all. I even worked with educators and wrote a curriculum to go along with the books to teach children math, science, music, and of course geography all based on PawPaw's adventures.

The photo I couldn't forget

It was around that time that I went to India. And saw the cages. And took the photo that changed my life. God wouldn't let me forget what I'd seen. The more I learned about the horror of child trafficking, the more I wanted to do something to stop it, but what? After all, I was a writer, not a rescuer. I'd published hundreds of news articles and three children's books and a companion curriculum for teachers—but I certainly didn't know how to stop kids from being sold for sex every night. Yet I couldn't forget. My board of directors encouraged me to narrow our focus to one particular cause, and I knew it was this one. Two months after that board meeting, I was on a plane back to Thailand researching what we could do and hoping I could find a way to make a difference. I secretly visited safe houses with fences around them and met with the directors and the children. I talked to teenage girls who had been rescued from forced prostitution. I interviewed the social workers and counselors

"David reigned over all Israel; and David administered justice and righteousness for all his people."

—2 Samuel 8:15 NAS

who helped them heal. I met with attorneys who worked to arrest traffickers and put them behind bars.

The entire time I was there I kept looking for where I could plug in. What was God calling me to do? What was the hole I could plug to stop kids from being trafficked? I filled an entire notebook with what I was learning—yet at the same time it felt as if God had a big clipboard and was crossing off everything He wasn't calling me to do. The list grew longer by the hour. Diana the social worker? Nope. Diana the attorney? Nope. Counselor? Law enforcement? Rescuer? Nope, nope, nope. Build a safe house for rescued girls? Nope, they'd have to implode it after I left. (Being handy with a hammer and nails is definitely not one of my strong points.) What in the world could I do to keep kids from being trafficked?

On my last day in Thailand I still didn't know what God wanted me to do. I wasn't panicking because I figured He wouldn't take me halfway around the world and send me home again without an assignment…yet the clock was ticking. My final meeting was with two social workers and an attorney. I gave them my laundry list of what I couldn't do.

"But I keep hearing that kids get taken because they don't know any better," I told them. In fact, I had heard the same story over and over again almost every day in Thailand: Kids get lured into trafficking because they believe the lies traffickers tell. Their parents do, too. They honestly trust the well-dressed "auntie" who shows up in the village offering to educate their daughters in the big city. "Just sign here," auntie says with a smile and the parents never see their

"We've bought into the myths collectively as a society that the girl is choosing it, she likes it, she's making a lot of money."

—Demi Moore

AUDACIOUS

"He saves the needy from the sword, from the mouth of the mighty, and from their hand. So the poor have hope, and injustice shuts her mouth."

—Job 5:15-16 NKJV

What's the big idea?

Your spiritual gifts—part 1

Spiritual gifts are what God gives you to get the job done. "We have different gifts, according to the grace given to each of us" (Romans 12:6 NIV). We're determining what exactly your "big idea" is, and one of the ways is to look at the spiritual gifts God gave you. So go to either of these sites and take the spiritual gifts test: www.gifttest.org (general) or www. kodachrome.org/spiritgiftyouth (specifically for youth and young adults). You can fill it out online and as soon as you click the "submit" button, you'll have an instant answer.

What did you score highest on? _____ Do you agree? _____

What else did you score high on? _____ Do you agree? _____

What did you score lowest on? _____ Do you agree? _____

What else did you score low on? _____ Do you agree? _____

What does this tell you about yourself? _____

Where does this mean God has gifted you? _____

Why do you think He wired you that way? _____

Remember, we're trying to determine the gifts God has already given you in order to accomplish the assignment that He's in the process of showing you. Just because you score low on something does not mean you're hopeless. You may not need that gift to get your "big idea" done.

daughters again. Instead their sweet little girls are sold from one trafficker to another. They might end up in Bangkok or Pattaya and lost in the lucrative child sex industry. Or they might be smuggled across a border and wind up in Malaysia, Brunei, or the Netherlands. Or Dallas.

"You already know what I can't do," I told the women I was meeting with, "but I'm a writer. I'm really big on awareness. And I've written children's books and curriculum. What if I write books for kids and curriculum for schools—can you use them?"

They smiled.

"Oh yes," one of the women replied.

"We don't have anything like that," said the other.

I had my marching orders. There was only one tiny little problem: I had no idea how to write a plot. Sure I'd written three children's books but they were for toddlers and there wasn't a plot to be found in them. I had no clue how to write one—so I learned how. I bought books about plot. I talked with writers, went to meetings, and went back to the library and perched on little chairs again reading little books while mothers once again eyed me suspiciously. I went back to Thailand to find out what needed to go into the book and curriculum. I interviewed the same safe house directors I'd talked with on the previous trip and anyone else who would give me the time of day.

A friend told me about something called the Hero's Journey—or what I call the twelve-step program for fiction writers. So while I was

17

AUDACIOUS

"If it is a matter of justice, who can challenge him?"

—Job 19:19 NIV

in Thailand I found an internet café, searched for "hero's journey," and downloaded it. Back at my guest house, I sat under a shade tree with the list and my notebook. Within an hour I had a plot. It's pretty much the same plot that is in the book today: Blossom is a caterpillar who has a dream to fly; in her quest to follow her dream she learns five important truths—the hard way, of course. She gets kidnapped by the dream thieves who are out to steal everyone's dream. The whole storyline became an allegory for trafficking.

I came home from that trip armed with not only my plot but pages of notes from all my interviews with safe house directors, attorneys, and counselors. My writer's group—Valerie Kosky, Karen Armistead, and Debbie Cole—kept me going even though some days they tore everything I wrote to shreds. Them: "You need more conflict." Me: "I've spent my life avoiding conflict! I don't want to write about it." I kept writing. To my great shock, what came out of my fingers and onto my laptop wasn't just a short children's book but a children's novel. I'd heard of this happening to other writers, but never expected it to happen to me. I just kept writing, and as the word count grew and grew I had no idea how I would get this book translated into hundreds of languages. But I just kept writing.

In 2007 a beautiful children's book called *Flotsam* won the Caldecott Medal for best children's book illustrations of the year. Illustrator David Wiesner told his entire story without words. Voila. Light bulbs went off in my head and God said, "Do the same thing. After you write the manuscript, then tell your story without words." When I finally finished my manuscript, it was 35,000 words. I turned it over to Leah who had illustrated my PawPaw books. Page by

"The Almighty is…exalted in power; in his justice and great righteousness, he does not oppress."

—Job 37:23 NIV

page she took my plot (yes, I really had one!) and turned it into a wordless book. When she finished, the wordless book had eighty pages with more than 500 individual illustrations.

This time I didn't even bother looking for an outside publisher but knew Born2Fly could publish it. I had all the experience from doing the PawPaw books myself and knew how to do it. I asked the same designer, Cathleen Kwas, to do the layout of this book, and had a printer in China all lined up when my writer's group called a special meeting with me. Actually I would call it more like an intervention. They gently but very firmly told me that I absolutely positively could not publish the wordless book without a curriculum because no child was going to read this allegory about a caterpillar with a dream to fly and say, "Oh! I shouldn't run off with a trafficker!" They told me it absolutely positively needed a companion curriculum so that teachers and parents could teach the important concepts in the book.

I was in tears. After so many years of hard work, I wanted to hold that book in my hand and get it to kids all over the world. My finances were in shambles. I had long ago realized I could not continue to do my own journalism and other writing and this; there was not enough time in the day to do justice to both and if I wanted Born2Fly to fly, I would have to drop my own writing so that I could focus on Born2Fly. I begged for whatever funds I could to keep in all going. There were days when I literally had no food in my refrigerator. God would regularly send someone with food or a check, but there were days when there was nothing. Our donors were more than patient with me and very understanding, but I'm

19

AUDACIOUS

"He will minister justice to the peoples."

—Psalm 9:8 AMP

What's the big idea?

Your spiritual gifts—part 2

In the previous "What's the big idea?" you took a spiritual gifts test that hopefully helped you understand how God has made you. There are a number of passages in the New Testament that list spiritual gifts. Look over the list below and put a + sign by the gifts you know you have and a - sign by the ones you know are just not you.

Romans 12:1-13
Encourager
Giver
Leader
Mercy
Perceiver
 (prophetic)
Server
Teacher

Ephesians 4:11-12
Apostle
Evangelist
Pastor
Prophet
Teacher

1 Corinthians 12:1-31
Administration
Apostle
Discernment
Faith
Healing
Helps
Knowledge
Miracles
Prophecy
Teaching
Tongues
Tongues
 interpretation
Wisdom

Other gifts
Craftsmanship
 (see Zechariah 1:20-21)
Hospitality (see 1 Peter 4:9-10)
Intercession (see 1 Timothy 2:1)
Martyrdom (see 1 Corinthians 13:3)
Missionary (see Ephesians 3:6-8)
Voluntary poverty
 (see 1 Corinthians 13:3)
Worship (music, dance,
 songwriting) (see Psalm 96:1)
Writing (see Psalm 45:1 and
 Habakkuk 2:2)

What does this tell you about yourself? Are you beginning to see any patterns about how God made you, what you love to do, what you don't like to do, and how He might use you to stop child trafficking? Write your latest understanding here:

_____

_____

_____

sure even they were wondering when I was actually going to publish this long-awaited book that would keep kids from being trafficked.

It was another long year before the curriculum was ready. In addition to Karen, I also worked with GeorgiAna Larson, a fantastic educator who had worked with at-risk families. She took it to a level that I never could have. The result was a six-session awareness and prevention program with separate tracks for children and teenagers. The five truths that Blossom learned became five sessions in the curriculum, and we added one more—a commitment ceremony where kids and teens make a commitment not to be trafficked. In everything we did, our goal was to reach kids before the traffickers do—to cut off the supply line so that kids never got trafficked in the first place.

We tested the curriculum and wordless book in five countries: in Thailand at one of the safe houses I visited, in Bulgaria at a summer camp for gypsy children, in Russia at orphanages for teens, in the Philippines at a youth project, and in the Dominican Republic at a community center for families. I traveled to Russia to meet with our test team there. The other countries invited me, of course, but with limited funds I could visit only one country; gone were the days when a magazine or news organization was paying my way. I had to raise every cent myself.

The test phase was a huge success and once we got feedback from the teachers and kids, we made final changes to the wordless book and the curriculum—and I had to decide how I was going to come up with the money to print and distribute the materials all over the

"I ask my brothers and sisters in faith and all men and women of good will for a decisive choice to combat trafficking in persons."

—Pope Francis

"The LORD is known by his acts of justice; the wicked are ensnared by the work of their hands."

—Psalm 9:16 NIV

Trafficked children

Miracles

It makes no sense to us. Why would a young mother and her two-year-old son blindly accept the invitation of a man they don't know to cross a border and visit another country?

That's exactly what happened to a young woman in Vietnam. The trafficker, Pham Anh Tuan, lured her across the border from Vietnam to China, where they visited the trafficker's aunt. Tuan quickly separated the mother from her son, and sold the child to a trafficking ring for 15 million Vietnamese dollars (U.S. $843).

Eventually a childless couple in another part of China paid a high price to adopt the boy. This is one of the tragic results of China's one-child policy, but that's another story for another book.

Tuan returned to Vietnam, lured a teenage girl to China, and brought her to his aunt, who sold her to a brothel for $843. Miraculously the girl escaped and returned to Vietnam. (If anyone escapes from a brothel, I consider it a miracle.) Miraculously the child and mother were rescued and reunited. (If anyone is rescued from traffickers, I consider it a miracle.)

Sadly this type of cross-border child trafficking happens regularly all over the world.[*]

* Police arrest human trafficker, Saigon GP Daily, May 14, 2009. www.saigon-gpdaily.com.vn/Law/2009/5/70767/

world. We certainly didn't have the half million dollars it would take to print books and curriculum and ship them all over the world. In fact, when I traveled to Russia I devoted an entire suitcase filled with curriculum and wordless books and had to pay excess baggage fees for the privilege. I knew we had to come up with a better way.

Suddenly I knew the answer. Every one of our test teams in all five countries used the materials digitally. We sent them PDFs of the wordless book and they either showed the book to small groups on a laptop, projected it onto a screen for larger groups, or printed it out locally if they needed a paper version. Ditto for the curriculum; the teachers just needed one copy on computer and they could easily print it out if they needed a paper copy. If it worked for them, I reasoned it would work everywhere else in the world, too. So I made the decision to distribute everything digitally—which also meant we could just give it all away. I knew most organizations around the world that work with kids couldn't afford to pay anyway. I uploaded everything onto the Born2Fly website, including the translations of the curriculum in Spanish, Russian, and one of the languages of the Philippines. Anyone who wanted them could fill out the registration form and once I approved them (and made sure they weren't traffickers themselves) I sent them a password and the URL for the hidden page so that they could download whatever they needed.

Within a few months of putting everything online, more than 300 organizations in more than sixty-five countries had already registered to receive the materials in countries like Mozambique, Guatemala, Australia, Botswana, Fiji, Nepal, and elsewhere around

"Tragically the world's oldest profession has one of the world's youngest workforces."

—Timothy Morgan

"Do justice to the fatherless and the oppressed, so that man, who is of the earth, may not terrify them any more."

—Psalm 10:18 AMP

Trafficked children

Sisters, sisters

Marina and her older sister were trafficked from Ukraine to Belgium, imprisoned in a brothel and forced into sex slavery (yes, one of the brothels that customers claim is filled with women who've willingly chosen this line of work—not girls like Marina and her sister who are brutally forced into it).

After six months Marina was finally allowed one call to her mother. When her mother didn't answer, Marina called a neighbor and learned that her mother was very ill and possibly dying. With nothing left to lose, Marina begged her captor to let her and her sister return home. He finally relented but would let only one sister go; the other had to stay.

For the girls the decision was agonizing but they finally decided that Marina should go; she was younger and more vulnerable. Before she left, however, the traffickers threatened to kill her sister if she tried to contact police or if she didn't return. They put her on a train back to Kiev with no luggage or documents and only $50. After a grueling journey traveling by herself, she finally made it home.

Despite the threats and risks, Marina knew she had to try to free her sister. She talked with local police who worked with law enforcement in Belgium to raid the brothel. After nearly three months, Marina's sister and the other women and girls were rescued and the traffickers arrested. The sisters were set to testify against their traffickers despite their fears of retribution, but before the case came to trial, Marina's sister died in a suspicious car accident.

Nine years later the case has still not come to trial, but Marina continues working for full prosecution of her captors. She has also started a non-profit organization in Ukraine called Path to Freedom that works to keep others from being trafficked.`

---

* Marina's Story: A Survivor's Fight against Human-Trafficking, IREX, www.irex.org/news/marinas-story-survivors-fight-against-human-trafficking

the globe. Kids went through the B2F program and the testimonies started trickling in about how they stood up to traffickers trying to lure them. We translated the curriculum into many more languages (Chinese, Thai, Hindi, and others) to reach even more kids.

One day I was holding a printout of the organizations and countries and the Lord told me, "You have the world's only database of anti-trafficking organizations." We are not exactly the largest anti-trafficking organization in the world but suddenly God had us networking groups together who might be working in the same country but had no clue about the existence of other abolitionists right in their own city.

A lot has happened since I took the photo that changed my life. Today Born2Fly is working all over the world—including on both sides of the border across which the girls in the cages were smuggled. On the India side of the border, we produce an anti-trafficking radio program heard every Sunday afternoon by more than 80 million kids and their parents. On the Nepal side, we work with a local abolitionist organization in Kathmandu that teaches our B2F anti-trafficking program in the very villages where girls are taken or sold. We're at work all over the world, but those two countries and that border between them is very special to me because of the girls in the cages.

When I took the photo that changed my life, I had no clue how to stop kids from being raped for profit thirty times a night. But God took what I already knew how to do—write—and showed me a creative way to help put an end to a horror affecting millions of

> "The greater danger for most of us lies not in setting our aim too high and falling short but in setting our aim too low and achieving our mark."
>
> —Michelangelo

AUDACIOUS

"For the Lord is righteous, he loves justice."

—Psalm 11:7 NIV

"I have need to be all on fire, for I have mountains of ice about me to melt."

—William Lloyd Garrison

children around the world. You might say, "But Diana, you were already a writer." Yes, and that's exactly my point. God didn't call me to build a safe house (remember? implosion?) or rescue kids or counsel them. He took what I already loved and in fact longed to do—write children's books—and created a way for me to do it that would make a difference in the lives of literally millions of children all over the world. The story is still astounding to me as I write this—but that's God. That's just who He is and how He likes to show off. He'll do the same for you. If you've read this far, maybe you're looking for where you can plug in. Maybe you have "justice" seared on your heart. Maybe you want to fight child trafficking, but you don't know how. Maybe someone has told you, "You're too young. Wait a few years. Wait until you're older. Wait until…" Fill in the blank. Maybe you've even told yourself that.

You just read my story. God is writing your story, too. He's the one who gave you that heart for justice in the first place and He has the exact place for you to plug in, using all the gifts and talents He's built into you. That's what this book is about—not just the horrors that kids around the world endure, but what you can actually do about it by using the passions He already built into your DNA.

The God of justice is asking you to partner with Him to shut down the global child sex trade—and He has already wired you to do that.

"The Lord loves justice."

—Psalm 33:5 NKJV

Be
audacious

You may be saying, "That's nice, Diana, but I don't want to read your story. I want to write my own—but I don't know how. I need help." That's what the rest of this book is about. You just read how God used what was already in me to help dismantle an injustice that I was passionate about. He'll do the same with you. You have your own story of passion and justice and what makes you angry and livid. I'm going to show you exactly how to partner with Him to do something about it.

You were born at the right time in history to do that. If you're in your twenties or thirties, you have a lot of labels attached to you. You're a millennial. You're a Gen Y-er. The title I love is the Justice Generation. You're a member of the generation that looks at all the hurts and injustices that my generation tried to do something about but frankly didn't do a very good job at. Maybe you were at the historic youth gatherings over Christmas break 2012: One Thing 2012 in Kansas City with 16,000 young people, Urbana 12 in St. Louis with 16,000, or Passion 13 in Atlanta where a whopping 60,000 students and young adults pledged to fight

"Your righteousness is like the highest mountains, your justice like the great deep. You, Lord, preserve both people and animals."

—Psalm 36:6 NIV

human trafficking. You have mercy and justice seared on your hearts—and possibly tattooed on your arms and neck, like a young woman I mentor. You're still wearing the tattered rope bracelet that a child slave put on your arm on a beach in Cambodia, like one of Born2Fly's interns. You risk your life with your undercover camera filming men buying children on a beach in Pattaya, Thailand, like another young woman I know. (You'll read about her later.) Is there any wonder why you're called the Justice Generation?

I can tell you all day that God has already put ideas and gifts and longings and creative strategies inside you—but maybe you don't see it yet. I can tell you that God has already put gifts inside you to get the job done—yet you need help to understand what they are and direction on how to put them into action.

There's a popular series of books for young couples who are about to have their first child: *What to Expect When You're Expecting.* It takes them through all nine months of pregnancy and tells them exactly what is happening, when, and why. The book you hold in your hands right now is your birth manual because you're about to give birth. Something has been growing inside you. It's time to welcome this justice baby into the world.

This is not an awareness book. You're already aware. Nor am I going to give you a list of ways you can fight child trafficking—because that would defeat my purpose for this book. I want you to come up with your own brilliantly creative ways. And you've already got them in you. I'm going to help you pull them out of you and then go beyond thinking about them to begin doing them.

"In your majesty ride forth victoriously in the cause of truth, humility and justice; let your right hand achieve awesome deeds."

—Psalm 45:4 NIV

When I first got the idea for this book and wanted to position it for your generation, I emailed and texted some of my Justice Generation friends living all over the world and asked for their reaction and advice. Here's what one of them said:

> "There is so much information [about child trafficking] and so many awareness books and even movies like *Taken 1* and *2*. We know the statistics and that it is a very real and disturbing business. What our generation needs is a book that can show us exactly how to be a part of the abolitionist movement. We are a generation of action. It isn't enough for us to sit on the sidelines. Prayer is something we are all familiar with. Prayer and fasting we got it…but now we need to know how to take traffickers and buyers out at their knees. So other than watching *Nefarious* and liking a zillion Facebook pages to show our favor of ending trafficking, what can we possibly do?
>
> "Write the book. We need to hear your heart. We need to be moved into how we can be fighters for freedom and redeemers for justice. Push us. We will go. We will do it. We just need frontline fighters like you to tell us how."

Those were my marching orders to write this book.

My new favorite word

It's *audacious*. I first fell in love with this word when I read *Good to Great*. Author Jim Collins explores qualities that take organizations from being merely good to spectacularly great, and one of them

"It takes a whole community to fight slavery. It is our collective fight to wipe slavery off the face of the earth."

—Laura Germino

"The heavens proclaim his righteousness, for he is a God of justice."

—Psalm 50:6 NIV

What's the big idea?

What would you do if money were no object?

I want you to dream big. Really really big. I'm not talking about child trafficking or any injustice. I'm talking about you. What would you do if money were no object? What would you do if you could do anything, go anywhere, be anyone? Tell me your dream. It doesn't have to involve stopping child trafficking—or any injustice. Describe it. _____

_____

Draw a picture of it.

What music on your playlist goes along with it? _____

What colors describe it? _____

What photos of it would you Instagram? _____

What emotion do you feel when you think about this? _____

_____

What food or dish best captures it?_____

What does this tell you about yourself? What does it tell you that you love to do? That you hate to do? What gives you joy? What bores you? What are you learning about yourself and how God made you?

_____

is having what he calls a BHAG—a "big hairy audacious goal." It's the goal that makes most people cringe, but the one you will sell everything to go after. Like the goal of stopping child trafficking. I fell further in love with *audacious* when I read this quote from Rob Morris, president of Love146, who was instrumental in helping me find what was already inside of me. You read his quote at the beginning of this book: "Ending human trafficking is not idealistic or naive. It is audacious. And it is people of audacity who change the world."

Does that sound like you? I hope so. *Audacious* means:

1   Extremely bold or daring; recklessly brave; fearless.

2   Extremely original; without restriction to prior ideas; highly inventive.

3   Recklessly bold in defiance of convention, propriety, law, or the like; insolent; brazen.

4   Lively; unrestrained; uninhibited.*

Please, I beg you, be extremely bold, recklessly brave, insolent, and unrestrained in your quest to dismantle the child trafficking industry. It will take all that and more. In fact we're going to look at nine keys to being audacious, which just happen to spell out the word *audacious*.

Audacious people dream audaciously and do audacious things to dismantle audacious injustices. Traffickers think audaciously so you

---

* Dictionary.com

"It is never too late to be what you might have been."

—George Eliot

"Endow the king with your justice, O God, the royal son with your righteousness. May he judge your people in righteousness, your afflicted ones with justice....May he defend the afflicted among the people and save the children of the needy; may he crush the oppressor."

—Psalm 72:1-2, 4 NIV

"Do one thing every day that scares you."

—Eleanor Roosevelt

need to, too. Train yourself to think audaciously. Everything in you and around you will try to keep you from this.

The Philippines has a very high rate of child trafficking. In one area so many kids are regularly snatched off the streets of the city that local law enforcement asked a non-governmental organization (NGO) if they could help teach anti-trafficking in the schools. One of the staff members of this NGO—we'll call her Laura—was all set to write her own anti-trafficking curriculum when she happened to tell a friend in the same city whom we'll call Anna. "You don't need to write a curriculum," Anna told Laura. "My friend Diana has already done that."

Can you see what I mean about God wanting to partner with you? How in the world could anyone have orchestrated that connection from thousands of miles on the other side of the planet? Anna and I go way back. She was in college when she joined a team I led to take bibles to the underground house churches in China. God so touched her heart for justice on that trip that she gave up a full university scholarship and eventually moved to the Philippines where she and her husband are doing community transformation work, including shutting down one of the most notorious garbage dumps in the Philippines. People live on the dumps—yes, in shacks built right on the burning refuse. Anna, her husband, and their team built a community off site so that everyone could move off the garbage dump for the first time in their lives, and they worked with the locals to create sustainable businesses where the people could work and provide for their families.

"Vindicate the weak and fatherless; do justice to the afflicted and destitute."

—Psalm 82:3 NAS

After Anna told Laura about B2F and our curriculum, Laura emailed me. We were actually looking for organizations to test B2F, so she agreed to be part of that phase. Her team taught the first B2F anti-trafficking class on a Friday. The following Tuesday in that same area traffickers snatched a little boy off the streets. A few days later they returned his body and dumped it on the sidewalk. All his organs had been removed (organ trafficking is another form of trafficking) and his head was cut off.

If you look up *audacious* on dictionary.com, there will probably be a picture of those traffickers. If they are a ten at audacious, then Laura and her team are an eleven. They didn't let that murder stop them. They continued holding classes. Laura is one of my heroes; she is definitely an eleven at audacious. She and her team have continued teaching Born2Fly, now well past the test phase. The local school district has given them permission to teach in all the area schools and they're well on their way to doing that.

By the way there's someone else who scored high for being audacious: the kids themselves. A few months after the kids went through the Born2Fly anti-trafficking classes, traffickers approached some of them and offered them cell phones if they'd come with them. We specifically cover that in the curriculum so these audacious little kids yelled at the traffickers, "No! We're more valuable than cell phones!" and they ran away.

So who out-audacioused whom? I give those kids an eleven. If you want to "take out traffickers at their knees," as my friend told me, you will have to be even more audacious than the traffickers are.

"If Plan A fails, remember you have 25 letters left."

—Anonymous

"Righteousness and justice are the foundation of Your throne."

—Psalm 89:14 NKJV

What's the big idea?

What looks for you?

"Jacob's well was there, and Jesus, tired as he was from the journey, sat down by the well. It was about noon. When a Samaritan woman came to draw water, Jesus said to her, 'Will you give me a drink?'" (John 4:6-7 NIV).

"Jesus sat down to rest and wait for lunch, but the Father had other ideas and brought a needy woman to Him," writes purpose coach Dr. John Stanko. "You seldom have to go looking for purpose. It almost always comes looking for you. God wants you to fulfill your purpose more than you do and that's why He brings the opportunities, people, and situations across your path.'"

John asks three questions that will help you understand God's calling and opportunities in your life:

1 Think about your life as far back as possible. What situation has repeatedly sought you out to be involved? _____

_____

2 What scenario or problem always finds you because you can help or have some answers? _____

3 Do you see any life patterns of things that always seem to find you so that you can be involved because God wants you involved?

_____

How do you think this relates to how He might be calling you to end child trafficking? _____.

---

* John Stanko, Pearl 31: Life patterns, January 31, 2013. http://www.johnstanko.us/2013/01/pearl-31-html

Here are some audacious quotes from traffickers who brag about their conquests:

> "On this trip, I've had sex with a fourteen-year-old girl in Mexico and a fifteen year old in Colombia. I'm helping them financially. If they don't have sex with me, they may not have enough food."
>
> —Retired U.S. school teacher (via U.S. Department of Justice)

> "If someone has a problem with me doing this, let UNICEF feed them."
>
> —Retired U.S. school teacher (via U.S. Department of Justice)

> "People are so much easier [to traffic] than drugs. The sentencing is a lot less, and you can just kick them and they'll do what you say."
>
> —Trafficker

> "They are merchandise because they are just pounds of meat."
>
> —Trafficker

Audacious much? Abraham Lincoln did not bring an end to slavery by being nice; he was audacious. William Wilberforce didn't shut down Britain's transatlantic slave trade by cowering in the face of opposition; he was audacious. It will take audacious twenty-first century people to confront audacious twenty-first century traffickers. It takes audacious and passionate people who look at this issue and say, "This far and no more. I'm drawing a line in the

"If everything seems under control, you're just not going fast enough."

—Mario Andretti

"The King is mighty, he loves justice."

—Psalm 99:4 NIV

Trafficked children

Trafficked in Washington, D.C.

If you still think child trafficking happens only in other countries, here's your wake-up call. In suburban Washington D.C., a man was sentenced to life in prison for prostituting a twelve-year-old girl to clients throughout northern Virginia, Maryland, and Washington, D.C.

Jose Ciro Juarez-Santamaria, a twenty-four-year-old illegal alien from El Salvador, met the girl after she ran away from home and asked for help in finding a place to stay. Instead the very next day he began prostituting her throughout the Washington, D.C. area.

He would take this child to locations where customers would be lined up waiting for her. He used alcohol and marijuana to keep her compliant—so that she would willingly serve dozens of customers day and night. We are talking about a twelve-year-old girl.

Remember, this didn't happen across the globe but across the street. And this is by far not an isolated event. Tens of thousands of children are trafficked in the U.S. He just got caught. Thankfully he's spending life behind bars as a result.*

---

* U.S. Attorney's Office, Eastern District of Virginia, July 28, 2011, www.justice.gov/usao/vae/news/2011/07/20110728santamarianr.html

sand and you cannot cross it. I'm going to do everything in my power to stop you. You can call me weird, tell me I'm obsessive, tell me to be realistic, but it's not going to stop me. If you're a ten at audacious, I'm going to be an eleven. I'm going to out-audacious you every time and I'm going to shut down your trafficking rings and free kids and keep millions more from ever being trafficked in the first place. And I'm going to bring you to justice."

Understanding: Forget it. If you want a map before you set out, forget it. You get puzzle pieces as you need them, not before. You're plowing new ground and it doesn't come with a map. I didn't start out having all the answers. My favorite line was, "I'm making this up as I go along." It did help to take what I knew and build on that and you'll have that small assurance too, but it certainly didn't mean I had all the answers—and you won't either. True, I was a writer, but I was a journalist. The only creative writing I'd ever done were three plot-less children's books for toddlers. Suddenly I was writing a children's novel and a curriculum to go along with it. There was a huge leap from the known to the unknown, but each step of the way God would show me what I needed for that particular step. For someone who is very organized and likes a complete to-do list ahead of time, that was a challenge. But it kept me leaning on God and that's exactly what I needed as I went further and further from my comfort zone into the unknown. In fact, one day a twenty-something friend called me up and said, "I was praying for you and I saw you and Jesus walking through a jungle. It was really dense and there was no path to follow, but Jesus was in front of you with a machete hacking away at all the brush while you were

"History shows us that the people who end up changing the world are always nuts, until they are right and then they are geniuses."

—John Eliot

"I will sing of your love and justice; to you, LORD, I will sing praise."

—Psalm 101:1 NIV

What's the big idea?

What would you do if you knew you could succeed?

Notice I didn't say, "What would you do if you knew you couldn't fail?" Why? Because failure is a part of success. If you're afraid to fail, you'll never take risks, and if you don't take risks, you'll never do anything audacious.

So what would you do if you knew you could succeed? This can be anything; it doesn't have to do with stopping child trafficking or any injustice. What would you do if time, money, or the time-space continuum were no object and you could always succeed at it? Describe it in as much detail as you can. You can also draw a picture of it.

walking behind Him with your hand on His shoulder. Does that mean anything to you?"

Yup. There were many days working on Born2Fly that I felt like I was blindly hacking through a dense and dangerous jungle with no clue where the path was. I can guarantee that whatever brilliant plan you come up with to stop child trafficking—and it will be brilliant—you'll regularly feel the same way. You'll feel like you're walking blind, but you're not. We'll talk more about partnering with God and what that means in two letters.

Dream Team. You need one. You can't do it alone and you don't want to. Surrounding yourself with a Dream Team is much more than just having a group of smart professionals who will help you actually get the job done. I'm talking about having a small, close group of trusted friends and family members who understand your heart for justice and will be your cheerleaders and encouragers when the going gets tough, and it will. A Dream Team who will build you up when others tear you down, and they will. A Dream Team who will speak life into your plan when everyone around you is telling you you're crazy and you should stop being so idealistic and get a real job, and they will. A Dream Team who will encourage you and cheer you on when most people wonder what exactly it is that you do all day, and they will. A Dream Team who will pray with you and war on your behalf when you are so discouraged that you want to quit, and you will get to that point.

Ask me how I know all this is bound to happen to you. It's not because I read it in a book somewhere. It's because I walked

AUDACIOUS

"The Lord executes righteousness and justice for all who are oppressed."

—Psalm 103:6 NKJV

What's the big idea?

Your personality profile

One of the tools that has helped me understand who God made me to be and why I think they way I do is the DISC personality profile. I'm an I/S (influencer/steady). You can take a free DISC profile here: http://www.personalitystyle.com or https://free.peoplekeys.com, which give you basic information. It takes about seven minutes.

What is your personality profile? _____

_____

Do you agree? Disagree? Why? _____

_____

_____

How do you think this might help you as you discover your big idea?

_____

_____

_____

_____

If you want a more detailed DISC profile that is like having someone read your mail, purpose coach Dr. John Stanko has offered to profile *Audacious* readers and give you a detailed report. Cost is $25 (normally $50) for a fifty-page personalized report, or $50 (normally $100) for a longer profile report that gives you information about how you work best, what motivates and demotivates you, etc. Contact him at johnstanko@gmail.com; let him know you're an *Audacious* reader.

through it all myself—and still am. Thankfully I have a small and trusted Dream Team that I can rely on and text any hour of the day or night, and they'll be there for me. You absolutely positively need that, too. You are taking on one of the most wicked forms of darkness on the planet and the forces behind it will not sit quietly by as you declare audacious war on them. Please don't go it alone. Begin making a list of people who can be a part of your Dream Team, people who care about you, support you and encourage you. It could be a teacher, a pastor, coach, family member, counselor, advisor, or close friend. And if you're married, hopefully your spouse. Spend some time thinking about your list and praying about the names on it. When you're ready, talk to each person about what you want to do and ask if they'll be on your Dream Team. Warning: Sometimes even your Dream Team won't understand you, and that's why you need to (please go to the next letter)…

Align yourself with the God of justice and He'll align Himself with you. He's the key member of your Dream Team. He's actually waiting to partner with you. He's the one who put the passion and fire inside you to dismantle the global child sex trade. He's the one who gave you the gifts and longings to do it. As soon as you turn toward Him, He'll be turning toward you.

One of my all-time favorite books is *The Artist's Way,* by Julia Cameron. It's a secular book yet it's all about God. Cameron's entire premise is that God is a creative God and He made us to be creative people—and He longs to partner with us to do that. She talks about "synchronicity," meaning when you position yourself toward God to do your creative endeavors, He'll send you the people, finances,

> "If you really want to do something, you'll find a way. If you don't, you'll find an excuse."
>
> —Jim Rohn

41

AUDACIOUS

"How blessed are those who keep justice, who practice righteousness at all times!"

—Psalm 106:3 NKJV

Audacious abolitionists

Artists using their art to bring healing

Art students at Florida State University (FSU) have come up with an innovative use of art to help victims of human trafficking. Art is often used to bring awareness of human trafficking—visual art, music, dance, theatre, photography—but this program goes way beyond awareness. It's actually using art therapy as part of the healing process that rescued slaves go through.

I learned about the program when I attended an inspiring exhibit of artwork created by men and women who were rescued from slavery in Florida. As part of their healing, they were offered the opportunity to participate in art therapy and share some of their experiences in creative ways. The artwork became an exhibit called Freedom of Expression: Art by Rescued Modern-Day Slaves.

My favorite pieces were seven mixed-media wall hangings created by a group of Mayan women that told the sad story of how they were trafficked from small villages in Guatemala and brought to Florida where they were forced into sex slavery. Their artwork took me on an emotional journey of their family life at home, the trauma forced upon them, their rescue, and their road to healing and restoration.

FSU's Center for the Advancement of Human Rights partners with the university's art department to create even more art-centered strategies to fight human trafficking. Each summer the center funds a program for two FSU art therapy grad students to work at a home in Thailand for children rescued from sex trafficking.

What I love is the creativity on both sides—the creativity of the FSU art students who use their own art to help others, and the creativity of the children, women, and men who use art to express their painful experiences and share them with the rest of us. If you're an artist, what creative strategy is God giving you to stop the traffic?

For more information: www.cahr.fsu.edu.

talent, resources, and tools you need to get the job done. You're actually syncing your life and matching it up with God's plans and purposes for you.

You must understand and believe that you are partnering with the God of justice. That is key. The passion you feel about child trafficking is because He feels that same passion and put it in you. If He's allowed you to feel it, and if He's allowed you to get angry about this injustice, why wouldn't He already have a plan to involve you in dismantling it? You must believe that is so in order to synchronize with His plans for you. If you don't think He has a plan for you, then you might as well close the book now and go update your Facebook status.

Counterattack. This is what happens when you decide to be audacious. Oh boy, I wish I could spare you the pain of this but it's part of the job description of being an audacious abolitionist. I wish I could tell you demons never showed up in my house. That people never told me I was crazy. That they didn't misunderstand and misjudge me, even those close to me. It happened to me and if you're going to be audacious, it will happen to you. Audacious people upset the status quo, and you will be making a lot of people uncomfortable, especially those who love "business as usual." You'll challenge them with your audaciousness. Some of them will come around to understand what you're trying to do, but sadly many won't. If you spend all your time and energy trying to please or placate them, you'll take your mind off the task at hand. Learn to spot who (and what) are the wet blankets in your life. What snuffs

"Silence in the face of evil is itself evil. God will not hold us guiltless. Not to speak is to speak. Not to act is to act."

—Dietrich Bonhoeffer

"The works of His hands are [absolute] truth and justice [faithful and right]; and all His decrees and precepts are sure (fixed, established, and trustworthy)."

—Psalm 111:7 AMP

What's the big idea?

What energizes you?

"I became a servant of this gospel by the gift of God's grace given me through the working of his power" (Ephesians 3:7 NIV).

The word for *power* in that verse is from the Greek word *energeo*, which is where we get our English word *energy*. "Your purpose is a gift and it comes through a divine working of His power in you," writes purpose coach Dr. John Stanko. "It also energizes you, so much so that you can lose sleep and not eat while functioning in your purpose and you can still be effective and joyful. What are you energized to do? What do you do that, when you do it, you sense God's energy flowing with and through you?"*

It's time to answer John's questions:

What gives you so much energy when you do it that you forget to eat or

sleep? _____

How do you feel God working through you with His power and energy?

_____

When or where do you feel His energy and power flowing through you the

easiest? _____

When do you not feel it? _____

How do you think this relates to what He might be calling you to do to end

child trafficking? _____.

_____ .

* John Stanko, Pearl 30: Divine energy, January 30, 2103, http://www.johnstanko.us/2013/01/pearl-30-divine-energy.html

out your passion? Who does? There are some people you will have to purposely remove yourself from.

In the end, it's you and Jesus. He's the only one who is truly going to understand what you're going through. He's the only one who'll see the long hours and sacrifice you'll be making. Even your closest friends, even your spouse, will not know the extent of it.

Beyond being misunderstood and even maligned by those around you, you will also experience counterattacks from the devil himself. Who else keeps these children enslaved? If his purpose is to steal, kill, and destroy, he's doing a pretty good job of it with little girls and boys being sold thirty or forty times a night, night after night after night. Do you expect him to sit idly by when you try to stop him? He's attacking you because you're being effective at attacking and immobilizing him. Otherwise he wouldn't bother with you. Zechariah 1:21 talks about "the craftsmen [who] are coming to terrorize" God's enemies (NKJV). Your craft—your art, your idea—can terrorize the enemy, and that's why he's so afraid of you.

Sometimes, however, you can do the devil's work for him. The most immobilizing counterattacks can come from you yourself. You can be your own worst self-critic. You can be the one giving yourself every reason why God couldn't possibly use you, why your plan stinks, why you'll never have the money to launch it, etc. That's too big; you could never do that. That's too small compared to what someone else is doing. You've got to learn how to silence the self-critic. It's his job to talk but you don't have to listen to him or agree

AUDACIOUS

"May victims of inhumanity and injustice not find us merely curious, but furious."

—Jamie McIntosh

"Good will come to those who are generous and lend freely, who conduct their affairs with justice."

—Psalm 112:5 NIV

What's the big idea?

10 things you've always wanted to do

Write down ten things you've always wanted to do. They don't have to be related to justice or anything spiritual. Don't think to hard about it. My goal here is to unlock your creativity so don't think too much about it and don't let the self-critic edit your list. Just write whatever comes to mind:

1 _____

2 _____

3 _____

4 _____

5 _____

6 _____

7 _____

8 _____

9 _____

10 _____

Which one surprised you? Why? _____

_____

_____

_____

with him. Helping you get through counterattacks is one of the best reasons to surround yourself with a strong Dream Team.

Ignore perfection. We always hear, "What could you do if you knew you couldn't fail?" but what about, "What could you do if you didn't have to be perfect at it?" It's the same thing, of course. You should not be focused on perfection; you should focus on moving forward. *Wait* is a four-letter word. If you wait until you have all the answers, until you have a perfect plan, until everyone is singing your praises, until you have all the money you need, you'll never dismantle trafficking. Perfection, after all, is an idol. It's pride. We want to do things perfectly because it makes us look, well, perfect. You can still do things with excellence, but perfection is an impossible goal. If you spend your time focusing on doing things perfectly, you'll never do anything. That's why audacious people are often misunderstood. They not only ignore the rules but they ignore perfection. And that upsets some people. But it won't upset the one you ultimately want to please: God. Don't focus on perfection but on moving forward. Make some progress each day, even if it's one tiny thing.

Open your eyes to see how God sees others. You can't tear down hate with more hate. You can only tear it down with love—God's agape love. Our goal is to stop traffickers, yes, but ultimately we want them set free, too. They're in a different kind of bondage than the children are and need freedom, also. Part of tearing down injustices is seeing how God sees others. The children are enslaved, but they are not slaves in God's eyes. We're proclaiming that as we work to set them free and keep others from ever being trafficked. Similarly we have to see traffickers as God sees them. He hates what

"Knowledge is the pathway from slavery to freedom."

—Frederick Douglass

47

AUDACIOUS

"I know that the LORD secures justice for the poor and upholds the cause of the needy."
—Psalm 140:12 NIV

What's the big idea?

Reversing the funnel

"Are you scared of your purpose?" asks Dr. John Stanko. "Many people are. They're afraid to do the wrong thing, so they do no thing. They've basically offered God what I call a funnel commitment. It starts out big at the top but becomes narrow at the bottom.

"Here's an example of a funnel commitment: 'God, I'll do whatever You want me to do—as long as it's in this country, in this region, in this city, in this neighborhood, in this church, at these times, and on these days and with these people. But, hey, I'm all Yours and will do anything You want me to do!'"

Can you see how you limit yourself with this mindset? Have you prayed funnel prayers? Write them here:

_____

_____

_____

_____

_____

How can you reverse that funnel? Write that here:

_____

_____

_____

_____

_____

_____

they're doing but He loves them. That's a difficult thing for a lot of people to swallow, and you may be one of them. Train yourself to agree with what God says about someone, not what the devil says about them. We see traffickers as traffickers and evil, but God sees them as how He originally created them and what He created them to be. If we see others that way, it's proclaiming their God-ordained destiny rather than their devil-ordained destiny. (Hint, this works for everyone.)

Undo unworthiness. This is sort of the Control Z or Apple Z button that you use on yourself. God has given you the honor, privilege, authority, responsibility, call, and mantle to proclaim and decree His justice to the oppressed. To do this you must believe:

1   He wants to bring justice to the oppressed. Do you really believe that or do you think He's powerless. Or stands helplessly by?

2   He not only longs to do this in partnership with you but that is actually His plan all along.

3   He thinks you're worthy enough to partner with Him.

What reaction does that provoke in you when you read those words? Do you feel unworthy? You have to learn to see yourself the way He sees you. You can't do audacious exploits if you think you're unworthy to do them. It's just false pride anyway. If there's something in your life that you need to clean up—a blatant sin that God is dealing with you about—then of course deal with that as soon as possible. If you're going after sin in another's life, you

"Difficulty is the very atmosphere of miracle—it is miracle in its first stage. If it is to be a great miracle, the condition is not difficulty but impossibility."

—L.B. Cowman

49

AUDACIOUS

"God…who executes justice for the oppressed; who gives food to the hungry. The LORD sets the prisoners free."

—Psalm 146:7 NAS

better make sure you don't have any hidden in your own. But if the only thing stopping you is a general feeling of unworthiness, then please deal with that. Honestly, it's pretty annoying being around someone who always feels like they don't measure up or they're not worthy. It's just false pride and just another way to call attention to ourselves. ("I'm the worst." "No, I am.") See "Ignore perfection" above. Then click that undo button and let's get on with it.

Stop preparing; start doing. Or in the words of Seth Godin, "Do the work and ship." It's good to prepare, plan, and strategize but at some point you have to take a deep breath and actually start doing the work you've been talking about for years. We all know people who want to read just one more book, take one more class, wait one more year. Child slaves are waiting for you to free them. You don't need to know much else.

I'm giving you permission to dream big dreams and to go do them. I ask you to be audacious. Be a world-changer. Dream big dreams so ridiculously audaciously beyond you that only God can help you accomplish them.

"He guards the paths of justice…then you will understand righteousness and justice, equity and every good path."

—Psalm 2:8-9 NKJV

How
much is
that girl
in the
window?

Kim stood on her side of the glass—the one-way window that allowed her Bangkok buyers to look her over while she played with the other girls. The other merchandise. At five years old, Kim wasn't the youngest child in the dank room. The new little girl just brought in this morning claimed that honor—a four year old who was crying in the corner. Kim looked at her blankly knowing it wouldn't be long before all the fight was squeezed out of her. After three or four nights of thirty or forty customers abusing and raping and viciously purposely sadistically torturing her tiny body, it didn't take long to realize the only way to endure the horror was to pretend it didn't exist. To check out mentally and emotionally. To keep the smile plastered on your face like this was everything you could possibly want in your five-year-old life. The smile that kept the johns happy and kept away the cigarette burns and the beatings from Mama. The drugs helped. Night after night of drugs kept the pain away. And the smile on her face. And kept her alive for another day. For what, she wasn't sure.

"A wicked man accepts a bribe behind the back to pervert the ways of justice."
—Proverbs 17:23 NKJV

"Your current
safe boundaries
were once
unknown
frontiers."

—Anonymous

Kim could barely remember how she got here. Way back in the hazy corners of her drug-laced mind, she remembered being back in her village with her family. She remembered a well-dressed woman showing up in the village. No one had ever seen such clothes before and who wouldn't believe someone of such stature? Auntie Su had wads of cash and gave it out generously, saying there was lots more where it came from—money to educate little girls in the big city. A kind donor was funding it. Just sign here, she said, and your daughters will have the education you never had.

Some mothers refused to believe such tales but others, like Kim's mother, put a big X on a document they couldn't read and said goodbye to their little girls, knowing they were sending them to a life they could only dream of. An education. A good job. A fine marriage.

Kim knew now it was all a lie. Every night the woman who said she was her new Mama told her she was a good little girl for earning so much money that was going back to her village, but Kim knew her family wasn't seeing any of it. The money lined Mama's pockets and bought her more clothes…and more girls. The supply line was never ending. Even when girls died from the trauma to their bodies or the older girls died from endless forced abortions, there were more girls out the back door. And more girls to sit in the window waiting for the horror to begin all over again.

▼ ▼ ▼

The bright morning sunlight made Abeeda squint as she left the orphanage and ran down the path past the other mud huts on her way to school. Mr. Chima had asked her to stay and clean up after

"It is not good to be partial to the wicked and so deprive the innocent of justice."

—Proverbs 18:5 NIV

the meager gruel that served as breakfast, which meant she was late, which meant the path was pretty much deserted—except for the man waiting next to the baobab tree. Just like every morning, he called to her. Just like every morning, she tried to ignore him. But this morning she didn't have her friends around her for protection. Suddenly he was blocking the path.

"No!" Abeeda screamed and ran back to the orphanage for help. Mr. Chima must have heard her cries and came out to see what the commotion was about.

"The man," she sobbed. "He's trying to get me!"

Mr. Chima opened his arms wide and let Abeeda run right into them. He held her protectively as she cried—and as the man came up to them. Brazenly. Right to the front door of the orphanage. The man reached into his pocket and pulled out a thick envelope. Slowly Mr. Chima loosened his grip on Abeeda and with a small deliberate motion he took the envelope—and pushed her into the arms of the waiting man. Abeeda watched in horror as Mr. Chima started to go back inside the orphanage and close the door. Her eyes pleaded with him.

He looked at her. He certainly didn't owe her an explanation but one spilled out. "The other children," he said without emotion, "they are hungry." He looked down at the envelope in his hands. "I have no other way…." and his voice trailed off.

For the rest of the day Abeeda was moved from person to person, and each time another envelope would change hands, growing fatter with each transaction. By nightfall she was smuggled across

"Given all the power and resources that God has placed in the hands of humankind, I have yet to see any injustice of humankind that could not also be stopped by humankind."

—Gary Haughen

53

AUDACIOUS

"To do righteousness and justice is desired by the LORD more than sacrifice…The violence of the wicked will drag them away, because they refuse to act with justice."

—Proverbs 21:3, 7 NAS

What's the big idea?

Your audacious idea

Right about now some crazy idea may be lurking inside you trying to get out—a creative never-been-done-before way to stop child trafficking, or rescue kids, or reach traffickers or buyers or sellers. It might be so crazy that it absolutely scares you. Everything inside you is saying, "That's just too crazy. I could never do that. Why would I want to? And what would my parents think?"

If your self-critic is giving you that much attention, then your idea must be outrageously audacious. Wonderfully audacious. In fact, I applaud you for your audaciousness.

So go ahead: Write down your audacious, crazy idea here. There's lots of space because you'll be coming back to this page more in coming days.

"For in the end, freedom is a personal and lonely battle; one faces down fears of today so that those of tomorrow might be engaged."

—Alice Walker

the border to a port town where she was put on a ship. She watched her beloved Africa fade into the distance. Late that night her grooming began. In the hold of the ship a dozen men took their turn with her. Abeeda who was so sweet and innocent. Abeeda who didn't even know what sex was.

A week later the ship docked and Abeeda was hustled off into the waiting arms of a woman whose white skin and yellow hair and unintelligible words scared her more than all the men on the ship combined. It was cold outside and white things were falling from the sky and Abeeda didn't have enough clothes on to keep warm. The woman pushed her into a car and threw a blanket around her, not to keep her warm but to hide her. They drove through the streets of the city and finally stopped at a decrepit building perched on the side of a canal. Abeeda could see children playing outside with their mothers. Why didn't anyone help her? And why couldn't she even scream? She kept fading in and out of consciousness.

Once inside the building Abeeda gasped to see a room full of girls just like her—girls with dark skin. Girls with the same horror on their face that Abeeda felt inside her stomach. Girls whose faces told her, "You are now the girl in the window."

▼ ▼ ▼

Benji's skin had once been so white and soft and pure. What four year olds' wasn't? But that of course was before the ropes and the duct tape and the chains that held him down. Long before the cameras. Long before the buyers that flew in for the weekend. Long before the drugs. Before the…

"The exercise of justice is joy for the righteous, but is terror to the workers of iniquity."

—Proverbs 21:15 NAS

Little Benji was too young to even remember anything before those days. He didn't remember his family, the camping trip to the lake the summer before, the way he had wandered off. He was too young to remember his mother's screams when she realized he was gone. Her desperate cries for help. The endless searches that found nothing but his little Teddy bear.

Atlanta was far from the lake. The apartment near the airport was a million light-years away from normal. For Benji, this was the new normal. The woman who clicked away on the laptop in the corner, talking into her cell phone, and arranging play dates for him. The men who flew in to see him. Others who paid online so the camera would send them images of the horror he was enduring. The men who came seemed to Benji like normal people. They told him they were—they were teachers and coaches and youth pastors and businessmen. They looked young enough to be his father—or old enough to be his grandfather.

Day after day, week after week, Benji stayed in the dark room. His white skin grew sallow. Still they came. Day after day, week after week. The woman would give him just enough food to keep him alive and occasionally she'd clean off the blood. After all, everyone wanted a fresh Benji. That milky white skin is what they paid big bucks for. For Benji, the boy in the window.

▼ ▼ ▼

Kim, Abeeda, and Benji are not real children but rather composites of actual children who are trafficked for sex all over the world. There is not one specific or unique scenario. "Children are trafficked into

"Those who danced were thought to be quite insane by those who could not hear the music."

—Angela Monet

"Rescue those being led away to death; hold back those staggering toward slaughter. If you say, 'But we knew nothing about this,' does not he who weighs the heart perceive it? Does not he who guards your life know it?"

—Proverbs 24:11-12 NIV

Trafficked children

Lori and her five month old

This is the story of a minor we'll call Lori living in Florida. She is a U.S. citizen, had some college education, and a five-month-old child. Lori borrowed some money from a man (we'll call him Greg) to help fix her car. She was slowly paying him back when she got arrested for shoplifting. Greg agreed to bond her out—but said she had to work for him to pay him back.

Greg posted Lori's picture online and sent her to prostitution calls. To make sure she would comply, Greg and his colleagues made her drop off her child to them as collateral while she went on prostitution calls. At the end of the day, she had to bring the money to them and they returned her child to her.

Eventually law enforcement brought Lori in for prostitution.* When she told law enforcement officers her story and showed them text messages confirming it, they set up a sting operation. The next time Lori met Greg to exchange money for her child, the officers arrested him and the other men and rescued Lori's child. Greg and his colleagues were charged with sex trafficking. Lori spoke at Greg's sentencing. The prosecutor asked for five to eight years in prison, but the judge was so moved by Lori's testimony that he sentenced Greg to twelve years.

People think they have to travel overseas to a third-world country and raid a brothel to rescue kids. You can if you want to, but really—just look in your own community. Kids are waiting to be rescued around the corner from your house. Read Lori's story again…be inspired…and then go help rescue someone. You can do it. Really.

---

* At the time, Lori was arrested for prostitution. However if that had happened after January 1, 2013, because she was a minor she would have been treated as a victim, not a criminal, thanks to Florida's Safe Harbor Law that went into effect that date. Numerous states are passing similar laws that automatically classify minors as victims of human trafficking, not criminals; that makes them eligible for specific services. Some states also have "vacate" laws, which mean any related crimes that were committed before Safe Harbor went into effect are removed from a minor's record.

the sex industry, for child labor, for their organs and body parts, for illegal adoptions, forced marriages, to be drug mules, or even to be groomed as suicide bombers," says Diane Hall, one of the coordinators of South Africa's National Freedom Network. Children are trafficked for hundreds of reasons and in thousands of ways. The methods, causes, and factors vary all over the world.

According to U.S. federal law, the Trafficking Victims Protection Act (TVPA) defines "human trafficking" as:

> The recruitment, harboring, transportation, provision, or obtaining of a person for:
>
> - sex trafficking in which a commercial sex act is induced by force, fraud, or coercion, or in which the person induced to perform such act has not attained 18 years of age; or
>
> - labor or services, through the use of force, fraud, or coercion for the purpose of subjection to involuntary servitude, peonage, debt bondage, or slavery.
>
> Coercion includes threats of physical or psychological harm to children and/or their families.
>
> Any child (under the age of eighteen) engaged in commercial sex is a victim of trafficking."*

Note that part of the definition: Anyone under the age of eighteen is automatically designated as a victim, not a criminal; force, fraud,

*U.S. Trafficking Victims Protection Act of 2000. www.acf.hhs.gov/programs/orr/resource/fact-sheet-child-victims-of-human-trafficking

AUDACIOUS

"In every generation it has, without exception, been those who dared to live with an irrepressible dream who changed history."

—Anonymous

"The righteous care about justice for the poor, but the wicked have no such concern."
—Proverbs 29:7 NIV

What's the big idea?

The self-critic

In the previous "What's the big idea?" you took a big breath and a big leap of faith and wrote out your crazy, audacious idea. I have no doubt that your own personal self-critic immediately gave you every reason on earth why that is a dumb idea, why you could never do it, and even if you tried you'd be laughed off the face of the planet. Let's expose that self-critic right now. Please write down every one of the reasons he gave you. No one is looking. Just list them all here:

What the self-critic is telling you: Leave this column blank for now:

1 _____   _____

2 _____   _____

3 _____   _____

4 _____   _____

5 _____   _____

6 _____   _____

7 _____   _____

8 _____   _____

9 _____   _____

10 _____   _____

or coercion do not need to be proved for minors. A victim does not need to be physically transported from one location to another in order for the crime to fall within these definitions. Trafficked children can be toddlers. They can be teenagers. Or they can be infants. Child trafficking happens in every single country of the world—including yours. Right now you're probably saying, "She doesn't mean my country." Oh, but I do. Let me repeat that: Child trafficking happens everywhere. Including your country, your state, and your city. Right this moment recruiters are organizing in your city. Right this moment pimps are at the food court of your local mall recruiting teenagers. They're already working in your middle schools. The recruiters are even kids themselves who are already lured into the trade. They may be living at home recruiting for traffickers. It happens all over the country. It happens not just in "that" part of town but in your part of town. (Why in the world would traffickers exempt your part of town?) Traffickers, of course, like you to live in the dark thinking they don't operate where they do. It makes their life so much easier.

It's impossible to draw a nice neat circle around the causes of trafficking. As you read in the three stories, there are many, many causes: poverty, greed, lust, convenience, and more. Human trafficking is the second highest-grossing illegal industry on the planet, after illegal drugs. There's very little risk, which is why organized crime is so involved. It's very risky to arrange for a drug drop but who thinks twice about seeing an adult walking with a child or someone talking with a teenager? It's also so lucrative because you can sell a drug once, but you can sell a child over and over again.

"Wisdom is knowing what to do next; virtue is doing it."

—David Starr Jordan

"Administer justice for the poor and needy."

—Proverbs 31:9 AMP

Trafficked children

Yesterday I met some slaves

More precisely, *former* slaves. Former child slaves from Haiti. Their stories got me—not just what they went through as slaves, but what they've done with their lives in spite of it all. Take Bill, for example. When he was just two months old, his father died. When he was six, his mother died. An aunt came to his small village and promised him a home and schooling in the capital of Port au Prince. He went with her, believing his life was about to turn around.

Instead at six years old, Bill became a restavek—one of Haiti's child slaves. Bill worked for his aunt, who severely abused him, and her family. There was no school for him. He didn't even have a bed. He slept on the floor and was the first one up in the morning and the last one to sleep. He was a slave for the family.

Yet Bill had a dream inside him to be a drummer. When he would walk to fetch water in large plastic containers, he'd turn the empty containers upside down and play them like drums. One day a nun discovered him at a market and got him out of the abusive family and into a home for boys called St. Joseph's. There he had a place to live and go to school—and people who encouraged his artistic talent. They arranged for him to study at a special program for drummers in the U.S. at Duke University. Eventually he went to Africa where he studied with the finest drummers in the world.

Today he is numbered among them—a world-class drummer who is now the director of St. Joseph's Home for Boys and co-director of the home's community art center and the Resurrection Dance Theatre of Haiti (RDTH). I watched a moving performance by RDTH—Bill now in his 20s along with other men and boys, including the youngest member of the troupe, nine-year-old Didi who stole everyone's hearts. I love RDTH because they have the same vision we do at Born2Fly—not just to rescue kids from slavery but to set them free to dream big dreams and be who God created them to be. Everyone deserves that.

Countries of the world can fall into three categories of trafficking. They can be source countries (where children are trafficked from), destination countries (where children are trafficked to), and transit countries (children are trafficked across or through them). Again, it's not a nice neat scenario. Most countries are at least two of those; some are all three.

Very few children are ever rescued from trafficking. Traffickers pay a lot of money for their merchandise—perhaps $300 a child, sometimes more, sometimes less depending on the country. They can make that back very quickly so they take great pains to protect their investment. It's very difficult to rescue a child because of that and even once a child is rescued brothel owners will try to steal their "possessions" back. Plus most children do not want to be rescued. You may find that unbelievable, but it's true. I once heard Sharon Cohn Wu from International Justice Mission say, "It's easy to rescue children who want to be rescued, but these children do not want to be rescued." They're so brainwashed and indoctrinated by their captors who've told them over and over again (with beatings to reinforce their words) that they, not law enforcement, are their protectors. They are the only ones who love them (and they beat them to "prove" it). Trafficked teenagers go through an elaborate recruiting and grooming process that involves not just breaking their will to run but bonding them to their captors. The very one who holds them in their power becomes their "Daddy." As one social worker told me, "It's a relationship. Prostitution is the price of that relationship." Everyone wants to be part of a family and traffickers go to elaborate means to create a family scenario with them at the

AUDACIOUS

"Learn to do good; seek justice, rebuke the oppressor; defend the fatherless, plead for the widow."

—Isaiah 1:17 NKJV

What's the big idea?

Silencing the self-critic

In the last "What's the big idea?" we let the self-critic talk—and I did that for a very important reason. Sometimes we need to ignore him but other times it's important to let him talk because he's really verbalizing what we ourselves believe. So now that you've written out every one of his reasons why your big idea is a dumb idea, let's go back and look at them. I want you to look at each one and figure out why it's a lie—and then write down the truth of God's word to counter those lies. If you know the truth, the truth will set you free. At this point in your journey you do not want to be held hostage by the enemy's lies about what God is revealing to you, so it's time to counter those lies with the truth of God's word—the bible.

Go back to the previous "What's the big idea?" and take each objection one at a time. In the right-hand column, write why it's a lie and then ask the Holy Spirit to show you the truth from God's word that will prove it's a lie. For example, if you wrote down, "I'll never have enough money," write "God promised He would supply all my needs according to Philippians 4:19" and "God supplies seed to the farmers, so He'll supply funds to me according to 2 Corinthians 9:10." If you wrote, "I'm afraid," write the truth that will counter it: "God didn't give me a spirit of fear but of power, love, and a sound mind, according to 2 Timothy 1:7."

You are replacing each lie with truth. The self-critic will always be talking but you can silence him with God's word.

top of the food chain. Can you see how a child's mind would be so messed up that when they are rescued, they often run back to their captors? Can you say "demonic"?

Those who are rescued often have to go through months of carefully building trust with the ones they were once taught to hate—law enforcement and other rescuers—so that they will even talk with them. Therapists must use specific methods just for trafficked children; a therapist once told me that the only other children with similar trauma are those who've been through ritual child abuse or satanic ritual abuse.

At the beginning of the previous chapter I told you that as you read this book God would be stirring up something in you—not just the anger you feel as you read these stories, but ideas and dreams and visions for how you can be part of His plan to bring justice to these children and to dismantle this multi-billion dollar industry. Perhaps you're starting to feel that now. Perhaps the dreams seem so outlandish that they scare you. Keep dreaming. Don't stop and don't let fear, failure, or unworthiness prevent you from hearing what God is trying to tell you.

I want to give you the 6 Ps of anti-trafficking work not only to give you hope that there are ways to dismantle this global industry, but to give you a grid for where your part fits in.

Protection is rescuing children, providing therapy and after care, and building safe houses where they can stay. This is particularly important in the U.S. where until recently there were only fifty beds

AUDACIOUS

"Within you right now is the power to do things you never dreamed possible."

—Dr. Maxwell Maltz

"He looked for justice, but behold, oppression; for righteousness, but behold, a cry for help."
—Isaiah 5:7 NKJV

What's the big idea?

5 smooth stones—5 reasons

Go back to "Your audacious idea" and read it over. Are you feeling audacious? Maybe a little worried? Maybe you're thinking the self-critic wasn't so far off after all? You just need to encourage yourself in the Lord, like David did (see 1 Samuel 30:6).

As you think about your audacious idea, list five reasons why God has called *you* to do this. Maybe it's something you learned about yourself by taking the gifts test. Maybe you realized something you've always loved doing that prepared you for this your whole life. Maybe it's something crazy you dreamed about doing as a child. Maybe it's a natural inclination or something everyone always compliments you on. Please don't be shy or falsely humble about it. This is no time for false humility, which is really pride. Just write down what God has already put in you to get the job done; you're bragging on God, not on yourself.

Reason #1: _____

Reason #2: _____

Reason #3: _____

Reason #4: _____

Reason #5: _____

in the entire country for domestic minor victims of sex trafficking, or DMST (that is, U.S. citizens under the age of eighteen).

Prosecution is going after the traffickers, building a case against them, and getting them behind bars. It's law enforcement and the legal community working together. It's also going after the buyers. And it includes changing laws as necessary or writing new laws.

Prevention is what Born2Fly does—cutting off the supply line of kids so that they don't get trafficked in the first place. Prevention involves awareness training not just for kids themselves, but for their parents, teachers, and communities. Another aspect of prevention is working to stop the demand; yes, some organizations have actually taken on this task.

Partnership is everyone working together to get the job done. Even competing pimps will work together to protect their investment, so we must work together with each other to stop them.

I've added two more Ps of my own:

Passion: Nothing is going to get done without it. Hopefully you're feeling more passion and anger with each passing chapter. You need that. I need that. This is a very difficult fight and we need our passion level increased regularly or we'll burn out. You also need commitment so that when the passion isn't there, you'll keep going.

Prayer: Nothing is going to get done without prayer, either. We're fighting a demonic spiritual battle and we have to stay close to God and listen for His commands, strategies, and whispers or the enemy will take us out.

"I can accept failure— everyone fails at something. But I can't accept not trying."

—Michael Jordan

AUDACIOUS

"With righteousness he will judge the needy, with justice he will give decisions for the poor of the earth."

—Isaiah 11:4 NIV

What's the big idea?

What in the world are you waiting for?

I mean seriously…what are you waiting for? You have a big idea; why are you waiting to begin working on it? You may have some very good reasons why you're waiting. They may be God reasons. Or they may be crazy fear-based reasons. Right now just write them all down; we'll sort them out later:

I need to wait before I move forward on my big idea because:

_____

_____

_____

_____

_____

_____

_____

Now read them aloud. How do they sound to you? Put a big "G" by the ones that are God reasons. Put a little "m" by the ones that are "me" reasons. What are some categories you can use to identify the "me" reasons (for example, fear, laziness, time, wanting perfection, wanting all the answers)? What else do you see? How will you respond?

What is God saying to you right now? Which of the first three Ps jumps out at you? And please don't choose passion or prayer. We all need those. Focus on the first three Ps. Which one makes your blood boil? That's a good indication of where God is directing you.

How did you feel when you read Benji's story? Abeeda's? Kim's? I hope their stories made you angry because they made me angry as I was writing them. My goal, of course, is not just to make you angry but to make you angry enough to do something about the injustice of child trafficking. Remember this book is not about awareness but action. Our premise—or what I will call our promise—is that God wants to partner with you to dismantle this horror and He's already put gifts, longings, plans, and more inside you to get the job done. So as you continue reading, be listening for His voice. He's speaking to you. Don't dismiss any ideas or thoughts as too big or too outlandish or too audacious.

"Often the difference between a successful man and a failure is not one's better abilities or ideas but the courage that one has to bet on his ideas, to take a calculated risk and to act."

—Dr. Maxwell Maltz

AUDACIOUS

"Fear not [there is nothing to fear], for I am with you; do not look around you in terror and be dismayed, for I am your God. I will strengthen and harden you to difficulties, yes, I will help you; yes, I will hold you up and retain you with My [victorious] right hand of rightness and justice."

—Isaiah 41:10 AMP

Trafficked children

Daughters who work so their fathers don't have to

If you haven't seen the film *Nefarious: Merchant of Souls,* a documentary produced by Exodus Cry about human trafficking and the sex industry, I encourage you to rent a copy asap. The producers filmed in nineteen countries in North and Central America, Europe, Asia, and the Middle East.

One of the most disturbing scenes in *Nefarious* takes place in Cambodia. In many other parts of Asia boys are more valued than girls, but here when a girl is born it's actually cause for rejoicing. Why? Because parents know their daughters will generate a steady supply of income when they're old enough to be trafficked.

"Old enough" means about four years old, by the way. The documentary includes an unsettling scene of a group of fathers in Cambodia playing cards and drinking—which they do all day, every day—all funded by selling their young daughters to sex tourists. The fathers don't need to work because their daughters do.

God's response: His heart for justice

What is God's response to injustices like the ones that Abeeda, Kim, and Benji endure? There are a bazillion scriptures about justice, injustice, a just God, a just people, and more. You'll see some of them throughout this book, but in this chapter I want to focus specifically on what we can learn about God's heart for justice from the book of Esther. This little book, which doesn't even mention God, is all about God's heart for justice—and the lengths He will go to in His quest to use ordinary people like you and me to dismantle entire structures of injustice. You may say, "Yeah, well, Esther was a queen." But she didn't start out as a queen. She started out as an orphan.

Esther's story takes place over a period of about ten years—from 483 to 473 BC during the time when many Jews lived in exile in Persia, or what is now Iran. They lived under an ungodly maniacal pagan king who frequently burst into fits of rage—and governed accordingly. He surrounded himself with ungodly men who hated Jews. And things were about to go downhill from there. Along comes Esther, a young Jewish woman whose parents had

"The Lord is exalted, for He dwells on high; He has filled Zion with justice and righteousness."

—Isaiah 33:5 NAS

both died. When King Ahasuerus decided to hold a contest for the woman who would be the next queen, Esther's cousin Mordecai encouraged her to join the competition. Every day he sat at the city gates listening for news of what was going on inside the palace. As a Jew, he refused to bow down in worship to the king's men, particularly the king's evil counselor, Haman. Whenever Haman passed, everyone bowed in homage—except Mordecai. It didn't matter to Haman that the rest of the city bowed; that one guy still standing totally annoyed him and enraged him. When Haman found out that Mordecai was a Jew, he decided to take action. He plotted to kill not only Mordecai but every Jew everywhere in the king's empire. That empire stretched from India to Ethiopia so we're talking millions and millions of Jews. Haman convinced the king to sign a death order against them. According to the law of the day, even the king himself could not reverse his own order. The death sentence against Jews all over the world was sealed.

But God. God used a young Jewish woman to work in partnership with Him to reverse the deal. I'm not going to tell you the rest of the story because I want you to read it yourself. Go ahead. I'll wait. The book of Esther is short—just about seven pages (in my bible at least) and you can read it in about twenty minutes. As you do, remind yourself that Esther was about your age, maybe even younger. Look what God did through a young woman living in a pagan, unrighteous foreign land. Imagine what He can do through you.

Even though the book of Esther never mentions God, He's all over it. What can we learn from the story of Esther about God's heart for justice and His response to injustice? Forty-nine things:

"Behold, My Servant, whom I uphold; My chosen one in whom My soul delights. I have put My Spirit upon Him; He will bring forth justice to the nations."

—Isaiah 42:1 NAS

1   God's justice will provoke a battle. It often makes people "angry," "furious," and even "enraged" (see Esther 1:12, 2:1, 2:21, 3:5). That's because…

2   God's justice is often opposed to the law and by the law. And…

3   God's justice upsets the status quo.

4   God's justice loves to work with young and inexperienced people without resumes. He doesn't require years of experience. The stars of this story of deliverance are an orphan and her inexperienced cousin (see Esther 2:7).

5   God's justice often brings quick results and provision (Esther 2:9). Once Esther gained the favor of Hegai, who was in charge of all the young women, he "quickly" provided what she needed.

6   God's justice will require you to go through a period of preparation. Esther went through twelve months of preparation before she even met the king (see Esther 2:12). She spent three days preparing her banquet for him (see Esther 4:15 and 5:1).

7   God's justice surrounds you with a Dream Team (see Esther 2:15). You may walk into the palace knowing no one and nothing, but God will bring the people to you who will help you.

"The best way to get started is to stop talking and begin doing."

—Walt Disney

73

AUDACIOUS

"He will faithfully bring forth justice. He will not be disheartened or crushed until He has established justice in the earth; and the coastlands will wait expectantly for His law."

—Isaiah 42:3-4 NAS

What's the big idea?

Who do you say God is?

Jesus asked His disciples, "Who do you say that I am?" (Matthew 16:15 NKJV). He's asking you the same question. Which of these statements about God do you agree with? Write "yes" or "no" by each:

____ God expects me to do right or not at all.

____ If God gives me an assignment, He'll show me everything I need to do it.

____ God wants me to work at what I'm doing. It won't always be fun.

____ By the end of the day I should be pretty wiped out from work.

____ I know God loves me, but I'm not sure He likes me.

____ There's always something more I can do. If I look for it, I'll find it.

____ God helps those who help themselves.

____ Money is the root of all evil. God hates us to focus on money.

____ God wants me to deny myself in order to help others.

What did your answers tell you about your view of God? Ask a few friends to answer these questions and then discuss your responses. Did you notice many of these questions do not have cut-and-dry answers? I simply want you to spend some time thinking about your image of God, how He reacts in certain situations, and what you think He expects of you—and then determine how accurate that is. Look up some of those faux scriptures. For example, does the bible really say that money is the root of all evil? That God helps those who help themselves? You may want to ask God if you got Him right nor not. And then you may need to apologize to Him for how you've portrayed Him!

8   God's justice surrounds you with a Dream Team that
    may not look like you'd expect it to. Sometimes they
    will be the people you least expect to help you. Esther
    was probably the only Jew in the king's court; she was
    surrounded by people who lived, thought, and probably
    ate differently than she did, yet God built a Dream Team
    for her in the midst of the court. How many young women
    have eunuchs on their Dream Team? Esther did. Hegai,
    the king's eunuch who was in charge of the women of
    the king's court, became her confident. She followed his
    advice and as a result she "found favor in the eyes of all
    who saw her" (Esther 2:15).

9   God's justice is not intimidated by numbers. The word *all* is
    mentioned numerous times in Esther 3:1-6. It all may seem
    hopeless but God's justice can turn it all around.

10 God's justice can result in civil disobedience (Esther 3:2).
    Mordecai refused to bow down to Haman even though the
    king had commanded it. Civil disobedience can take many
    different forms and does not have to be violent (Martin
    Luther King, Jr., Gandhi, etc.), although often it is.

11 God's justice can cause you great anguish (see Esther 4:4
    and 8:6).

12 God's justice works in partnership with God's people. He
    usually doesn't make decrees or institute them apart from
    us (see Esther 4:14).

"It is good to create good plans and to set goals. Working on them and getting results is much better."

—John Delavera

AUDACIOUS

"But this is a people plundered and looted, all of them trapped in pits or hidden away in prisons. They have become plunder, with no one to rescue them; they have been made loot, with no one to say, 'Send them back.'"

—Isaiah 42:22 NIV

Trafficked children

Girls who vanish

Maria, a sixteen-year-old Mexican girl, met a young man who promised her the world. She believed the lies and went with him, but instead of a dream life she received nothing but pain. She was raped, drugged and sold for sex. In case she had any thoughts of running away, this is what the men did to dissuade her: "They took a gallon of gasoline and started pouring it over a girl," Maria said. "One of the men told me, 'If you don't do as I say I will do the same to you.' I wanted to look away, but they didn't let me. Even though the girl was on fire they kept hitting her and they were laughing as if they were enjoying what they were doing.'"

Another young Mexican girl, Rosa, was just fourteen when a man offered her a good job in the U.S. "My parents didn't want me to go, but I persuaded them. A week later, I was smuggled in to the U.S. through Texas to Orlando, Florida. The men told me that my employment would consist of having sex with men for money. I had never had sex before.

"And so my nightmare began. Because I was a virgin, the men decided to initiate me by raping me again and again to teach me how to have sex. Over the next three months, I was taken to a different trailer every fifteen days. I cannot forget what has happened. I was a decent girl in Mexico. I used to go to church with my family. I only wish none of this had ever happened.'""

Maria and Rosa escaped but there are thousands more girls like them caught in the vast, organized cross-border trade between Mexico and the U.S.—a trade in children and babies. Please understand these babies are not for adoption. They are part of the child sex trade. Yes, babies.

* Human Trafficking in Mexico Targets Women and Children, CNN, http://edition.cnn.com/2010/WORLD/americas/01/13/mexico.human.traffic.drug/index.html
** And so my nightmare began, author's blog, June 12, 2008. http://dianascimone.typepad.com/diana_scimone/2008/06/and-so-my-nightmare-began.html

13 God's justice gives you overwhelming assurance that He will right the wrong—even when you don't have a clue how that will happen. Mordecai told Esther, "Relief and deliverance will arise for the Jews" (Esther 4:14). He knew God would deliver them; he just didn't know how or through whom (at that point in the storyline, Esther hadn't said "yes" yet).

14 God's justice gives you a plan but it usually tells you only as much about that plan as you need at that moment (see Esther 4:16). It calls you, anoints you, sets you apart, leads you, and partners with you—usually without giving you any more information than you need. Esther didn't have all the answers at the beginning. It's the CIA principle: "People need to know only what they need to know." God tells you only what you need to know at the moment. Otherwise you wouldn't need Him. It's called faith. Remember the "u" in audacious?

15 God's justice gives you miraculous favor in high places, or wherever you need it (see Esther 5:1-2).

16 God's justice clothes you with royal robes (see Esther 5:1 and 6:10-11).

17 God's justice calls you to inner courts and high places, and gives you favor in the sight of those in power (see Esther 5:2).

> "How wonderful it is that nobody need wait a single moment before starting to improve the world."
>
> —Anne Frank

"My arm will bring justice to the nations."

—Isaiah 51:5 NIV

What's the big idea?

Where is fear controlling you?

In the past, what decisions have you made that are fear-based?

_____

_____

What were the consequences of those decisions? _____

_____

How is fear keeping you from your big idea?_____

_____

Can you see how fear has controlled you? _____

_____

What could you do to change that? _____

_____

_____

What will you do to change that? _____

_____

_____

When will you do it? _____

_____

_____

18 God's justice is concerned with what troubles you (see Esther 5:3).

19 God's justice gives you access to unlimited funds that He has set aside to dismantle injustice. Esther used the king's treasury to prepare two lavish banquets (see Esther 5:4, 8). The wealth of the wicked is stored up for the just (see Ezekiel 7:20-22, Proverbs 28:8, Job 27:13, 16-17, Ecclesiastes 2:26) so God's justice will release it to you. Even the wages of traffickers are stored up for you (see Isaiah 23:18).

20 God's justice won't let you sleep when you learn about an injustice. In the middle of the night, the king couldn't sleep (see Esther 6:1) and asked someone to read some boring old history books to him (probably so that he could fall back asleep). In the process, God brought to his attention a time that Mordecai had saved the king's life. Nothing had ever been done to honor Mordecai for his righteous actions, but that was about to change.

21 God's justice will cause people (even unbelievers) to remember the good things you've done (see Esther 6:1.)

22 God's justice will hide you if necessary as you partner with Him to fight injustice. Hamen found out in Esther 3:4 that Mordecai was a Jew, yet God kept the fact that Esther was a Jew from Hamen, the king, and everyone else in the palace. No one knew until she told the king in Esther 7:4. God protected her and her people.

"I am always doing that which I cannot do, in order that I may learn how to do it."

—Pablo Picasso

79

AUDACIOUS

"Now the LORD saw, and it was displeasing in His sight that there was no justice."

—Isaiah 59:15 NAS

"The problems of the world cannot possibly be solved by skeptics or cynics whose horizons are limited by obvious realities. We need men and women who can dream of things that never were."

—John F. Kennedy

23 God's justice results in a transfer of wealth from those who deny justice to those who work for it. After the king hanged Haman, he gave Haman's house to Esther and put Mordecai in charge of it (see Esther 8:1-2). Haman was a very wealthy man; remember, he offered to deposit 330 tons of silver into the king's treasury if the king would sign an order to destroy all the Jews (see Esther 3:9).

24 God's justice results in faith even when a death order is in effect. Between the time the king gave his original order to kill all the Jews but before his second decree went into effect that Jews could defend themselves, here is what happened: "The Jews had light and gladness, joy and honor. And in every province and city, wherever the king's command and decree came, the Jews had joy and gladness, a feast and a holiday." (Esther 8:16 NKJV). Remember, the day still had not come for the Jews to fight; in the natural they did not know how it would turn out, but they knew by the Spirit.

25 God's justice causes unbelievers to believe in Him. As a result of Esther's actions to save her people from destruction, "many among the peoples of the land became Jews" (see Esther 8:17). How amazing is it that while the death sentence was in effect against the Jews, people were converting to Judaism. That's faith and favor.

"This is what the LORD says: 'Maintain justice and do what is right, for my salvation is close at hand and my righteousness will soon be revealed.'"

—Isaiah 56:1 NIV

26   God's justice causes your enemies to fear you. In fact, you may start out afraid of your enemies, but God's justice will reverse it so that they are afraid of you (see Esther 9:2-3).

27   God's justice causes high officials who once persecuted you for being righteous to now help you. Even commanders of armies who were once against you will help you (see Esther 9:3).

28   God's justice will result in a continual increase of your power and authority (see Esther 9:4).

29   God's justice brings "words of peace and truth" from the throne (Esther 9:30). These words counter the words of the enemy that bring injustice and result in the "city thrown into confusion" (Esther 3:5).

30   God's justice elevates you from obscurity to places of unlimited power so that you can right wrongs (see Esther 10:3).

31   God's justice allows you to affect the welfare of your entire nation (see Esther 10:3).

32   God's justice doesn't operate on your timetable. It may seem like it's taking its sweet time, but when it moves, it moves "quickly." The death order against all the Jews was signed, sealed, and delivered, yet within twenty-four hours look what happened: Esther prepared two banquets, Haman was enraged that Mordecai didn't bow down to him, Haman decided to build gallows—and built them.

"Whether you think you can or whether you think you can't, you're right."

—Henry Ford

"I, the LORD, love justice."

—Isaiah 61:8 NAS

Trafficked children

Negotiating the sale of a three year old

A colleague who is a filmmaker visited Pattaya, Thailand, where child sex trafficking is not only rampant but often right in the open. She was there to take secret video footage of wanted pedophiles and report them to law enforcement. (You read a little about her in chapter six—Stephanie.) Here's what Stephanie wrote me:

"At first I was worried that I wouldn't find any possible traffickers or pedophiles to film, but it was quite the opposite. There was an abundance of sex tourists. With such a tiny camera it seemed impossible to film them all. Amidst all the Caucasian men, I quickly realized that, being the only Caucasian woman, just my presence was a threat to them. In fact, later as I reviewed my film I realized some of them had even followed me.

"After filming for many days, I took a night off to go to a festival with some friends. As I was walking back from a fun, carefree night, I passed a dark parking lot adjacent to an abandoned building where two men were talking. With them was a small girl, possibly European and no older than three years old.

"The men looked European as well and they fearfully glanced my way. At a time when I least expected, I found myself witnessing firsthand the negotiation and sale of this innocent little girl.

"From behind the street light I searched for her but the parking lot was dark, quiet, and empty. I never saw her again…but I couldn't forget her if I tried. My heart was officially wrecked.

"Quickly I ran to my hotel. Once in my room I fell to the floor against the door and wept uncontrollably. My doubts were no more. None of what I saw that night made it on film but it is engraved permanently in my mind. Since that night I feel haunted by the sick memory of greed that would ravage something so innocent as a means of profit.*

_____

* Negotiating the sale of a three year old, author's blog, April 5, 2011, http://dianascimone.typepad.com/diana_scimone/2011/04/the-negotiation-and-sale-of-a-3-year-old.html

Still within that twenty-four hour period, the king couldn't sleep, learned that Mordecai's good deed of years ago had gone un-rewarded, Haman happened to be coming into the palace right then, Haman was forced to honor Mordecai, Esther exposed Haman's evil plot, and the death decree against the Jews was reversed. All that happened in twenty-four hours. It almost takes longer to retell the story!

33   God's justice hears the cries of the oppressed.

34   God's justice means He surrounds Himself with people who have His same heart for justice. (Ditto for the opposing side; those who love injustice surround themselves with like-minded people.)

35   God's justice takes what is already in you and crafts a plan to dismantle injustice. It took Mordecai's skill as a mentor and his position as Esther's guardian, and took Esther's great beauty and audaciousness, and used them to bring her before the king, win his heart, and save a condemned people.

36   God's justice loves using beauty to dismantle the ugliness of evil. God's justice will often be a juxtaposition of beauty and horror. God used Esther's beauty, oil, cosmetics and more to tear down the ugliness of anti-Semitism.

AUDACIOUS

"The LORD God will cause rightness and justice and praise to spring forth before all the nations."

—Isaiah 61:11 AMP

What's the big idea?

Take your own reconnaissance mission

I hope you're so excited by the time you've reached this point in the book that you're ready to explode. I hope your head and heart are filled with so many brilliant and creative ideas that you can't wait to get started on them. I hope you're feeling so audacious that you can barely stand it.

No? That's all right. I was at the same point. Remember my reconnaissance mission to Thailand? I went there not only to learn about trafficking but also to learn what I could do to stop it. While I was there, God had His clipboard and crossed off all the things He wasn't calling me to do…and I was left with what He was calling me to do.

It's time for you to take your own reconnaissance mission. You don't even have to leave the country physically. Google a few words about your big idea and just keep following the links. Read as much as you can. Do it intentionally. Have your own clipboard. See what jumps out at you and intentionally listen for God's voice directing you.

What are you learning about your big idea? _____

_____

_____

_____

_____

_____

_____

37 God's justice will raise up Mordecais to protect and promote girls and women, Mordecais who refuse to bow down to idols.

38 God's justice can put you in the unusual position of serving with or even over ungodly people, evil rulers, and hostile ones.

39 God's justice gives you unprecedented access and the ear of those in high places.

40 God's justice focuses on the big picture.

41 God's justice focuses on the one.

42 God's justice results in miracles. Even when all seems lost and impossible, God's justice says, "Just watch." Mordecai and Esther (like Daniel and Joseph) faced death sentences against them, but God's heart for justice worked miracles on their behalf.

43 God's justice can reverse even an irreversible death sentence. Every single Jew in the entire kingdom was doomed to die on a specific day and there was no way to reverse the king's decree. Even the king himself could not change it. Yet God's justice provided a way.

44 God's justice will sometimes keep you hidden. You will feel like nothing is happening and that injustice is ruling, but He is working on your behalf behind the scenes—and He's

"Progress always involves risks. You can't steal second base and keep your foot on first."

—Frederick B. Wilcox

AUDACIOUS

"I am the LORD who exercises lovingkindness, justice and righteousness on earth; for I delight in these things."

—Jeremiah 9:24 NAS

What's the big idea?

The 4 Ps: Which one jumps out at you?

Here are four of the six Ps of fighting child trafficking. See page 67 for descriptions, although I'm not including passion or prayer here because you need them both no matter what your big idea involves.

1 Prosecution

2 Protection

3 Prevention

4 Partnership

Which one jumps out at you? Why? _____

_____

_____

_____

_____

_____

Which ones does your big idea fall under? _____

_____

_____

_____

_____

_____

keeping you hidden in the process. At the same time He is exposing wickedness in high places.

45 God's justice will always trump the law because God's justice is based in mercy, not legalism. Mercy always triumphs over judgment.

46 God's justice demands a celebration. For thousands of years Jews have celebrated how God used Esther to save her entire people from a death decree. Even during the Holocaust in the darkest concentration camps, Jews recited the book of Esther from memory to commemorate what God had done—and to encourage themselves that if He did it for Esther, He would do it for them. Interestingly, the bible says that not only Jews are to celebrate what is today known as the feast of Purim, but all those who ally themselves with them (see Esther 9:27).

47 God's justice isn't scared by the odds. One person + God = the best odds.

48 God's justice not only rights wrongs but in the process dismantles entire structures that are propping them up—political, cultural, legal, and more.

49 God's justice always leads to freedom.

Spend some time thinking about what you've read about God's heart for justice. What surprised you? What lined up with what you were already feeling deep in your own heart? What challenged you?

"A minister cannot preach the glories of heaven while ignoring social conditions in his own community that cause [people] an earthly hell."

—Martin Luther King, Jr.

"Administer justice every morning; rescue from the hand of the oppressor the one who has been robbed."

—Jeremiah 21:12 NIV

"211 degrees
Fahrenheit
is hot water.
212 degrees
Fahrenheit
moves a train."

—Anonymous

Can you see how the God of justice has already put His heart for justice inside you? Can you see that's not only normal, but part of His plan for the earth? Are you beginning to believe that just as He took an obscure orphan girl and elevated her to queen over a pagan nation, and in the process partnered with her to save her entire people from a death sentence—maybe He wants to use you to save millions of children from bondage?

Remember our line about audacious people in the previous chapter: "Audacious people dream audaciously and do audacious things to dismantle audacious injustices." You can keep telling yourself, "I'm not worthy, I'm not worthy," but that's just false humility. If you focus on that, you'll always say "no" to God. And by default, you are saying "yes" to the devil. But if you focus on God, like Esther did, you'll say "yes" to the plans He has for you. The enemy will never ever in the history of the entire world stop telling you're not worthy enough, prepared enough, rich enough, strong enough, beautiful enough, smart enough, or _____ [fill in the blank] enough. If you want to be audacious, eventually you will have to make the decision to stop agreeing with what the devil says about you and start agreeing with what God says about you.

Esther did. Will you?

"Do justice and righteousness."

—Jeremiah 22:3 NAS

Change agents

When you want to know the temperature in your home, you check the thermometer. When you want to change the temp in your home, you switch the thermostat. Thermometers change according to the atmosphere around them. Thermostats change the atmosphere. Which do you want to be? Do you want to just reflect what's happening around you, or do you want to be someone who actually changes it? A lot of people around you are seeing the same injustices you're seeing. Okay, some aren't; they're blind to everyone but themselves. Others genuinely do see the problems but really don't think they can do anything about them. "Let the professionals handle that," they reason. And they go on with their lives. And the injustices around them go on, too. That's not you, is it? You see what's happening around you and you're not only angry but you're passionate to do something about it. You're desperate to be a thermostat and change the atmosphere around them. As we begin this chapter you may be getting some inklings about what you can do, or maybe you still don't have a clue, or maybe you're somewhere in between.

"Woe to him who builds his palace by unrighteousness, his upper rooms by injustice, making his own people work for nothing, not paying them for their labor."

— Jeremiah 22:13 NIV

What's the big idea?

Your dream team

We all need friends and family to help us pursue our dream—our big idea. God has surrounded you with some of those people and you're about to discover others. List here the people who care about you, support you, and encourage you, people who will help you and advise you as you pursue your big idea. You could include friends, family members, spiritual leaders, teachers, coaches, business partners, counselors, advisors, or any special trusted person who can be part of your dream team.

_____   _____

_____   _____

_____   _____

_____   _____

Now list people you don't know but would like to get to know and add to your Dream Team. These are people who have some of the job skills and experience you might call on as you work on you big idea.

_____   _____

_____   _____

_____   _____

_____   _____

What can you do to connect with them?

_____

_____

_____

In this chapter we're going to talk about what some thermostats are doing around the world to end child trafficking. Remember our promise: The God of justice has already put creative solutions inside you to help end the injustice that you see. My goal in this chapter is to show you the creative ideas of others in order to spark a creative flame in you. As you read this chapter, intentionally listen for God's voice. He's probably not going to come with a drum roll announcing His presence. You may hear an audible voice, but more probably He'll just start dropping ideas on you. Please do not dismiss them. Do not do the devil's work for him. The further you read, the more the devil is going to do everything he can to tell you your ideas are crazy. If you listen to him it will be a lot harder to hear God. Here are a few tips on how to tell who's speaking to you: The devil will give you every reason why your idea is dumb. God will give you every reason why your idea is great. The devil will always try to discourage you and stop you. God will always encourage you and tell you to keep going. The devil always yells at you. God usually whispers. Will God give you a green light for every single idea you come up with? Of course not. But that's part of the process. You come up with the ideas, run them by God, and listen for His direction. The further you go on in this adventure, the easier it will be to distinguish between His voice and the devil's. And the more critical.

"I just keep buying fabric," my friend Jean said to me. "I'm not sure what to do with it so I keep making comforters. By the way is there anything I can do to help you with Born2Fly?"

"If at first the idea is not absurd, then there is no hope for it."

—Albert Einstein

AUDACIOUS

"He defended the cause of the poor and needy, and so all went well. Is that not what it means to know me? declares the LORD."

— Jeremiah 22:16 NIV

What's the big idea?

What's standing between you and your dream?

What is standing between you and your big idea? It could be mindsets, things, lack of things, people, etc. Write these in the left column:

_____   _____   _____

_____   _____   _____

_____   _____   _____

_____   _____   _____

_____   _____   _____

_____   _____   _____

How many of the things you listed have to do with you? In the middle column, write "me." How many have to do with others? In the middle column, write "others." What can you do to keep those people, mindsets, or things from stopping you? Write that in the third column.

Meanwhile my friend Rebecca loved giving tea parties. She homeschooled her son and worked part-time at a tea room. "Is there anything I can do to help you with Born2Fly?"

One of my contacts in Thailand ran a safe house for women and girls rescued from trafficking. I'd met Jillian (not her real name) on a previous trip and she introduced me to a lot of the young ladies who were very anxious to practice their English. After we ate dinner and the girls cleaned up the dishes, Jillian took me outside and showed me a wooded area where she was expanding the home. "We're taking in twelve more girls and this is where we're going to build an addition to the house," she said. At that moment we were standing in the middle of a muddy field full of trees, weeds, and debris. I knew she was seeing the finished building that would house girls on their journey to healing, but honestly all I could see was mud and lots of trees. Even more discouraging to me was the fact that this city had thousands and thousands of young women still enslaved. Rescuing a mere twelve of them seemed like a drop in the bucket to me.

"How do you keep from getting discouraged?" I asked.

Jillian turned and looked at me like I was crazy. "If I do what I'm supposed to do," she said matter-of-factly, "and you do what you're supposed to do, the job will get done." And that was that.

Her job was to build the home that would house twelve girls. My job was to go home, talk to my friend who had no idea why she kept making comforters, to my friend who loved giving tea parties, and come up with a plan. Within a few months we had one—a tea party

"The moment of enlightenment is when a person's dreams of possibilities become images of probabilities."

—Vic Braden

93

AUDACIOUS

"Behold, the days are coming, declares the LORD, when I will raise up for David a righteous Branch; and He will reign as king and act wisely and do justice and righteousness in the land."

—Jeremiah 23:5 NAS

Audacious abolitionists

Digging wells

Back in early 2006 when I knew Born2Fly wanted to get involved with the fight to stop child trafficking, I talked with Rob Morris, co-founder of Love146. Rob told me about villages on the border of Cambodia and Thailand where little girls walk long distances from their villages to the nearest wells. Child traffickers know their routes.

It doesn't take much planning to find a little girl walking by herself. And voila— another innocent child joins the worldwide trafficking trade. Her destiny is to be raped for profit twenty or thirty times a night for the rest of her life. All because she had to walk to find water.

Rob told me how Love146 was working to dig wells in these high-risk villages so that little girls didn't have to walk far to get water. In the villages where they'd dug wells, the rate of trafficking was going down. And girls could spend time in school instead of lugging water jugs. No water = child trafficking. Water = No child trafficking. "The children in those communities are now in school and getting an education," Rob later emailed me. "No longer prey for traffickers."

This isn't just a problem on the Thai/Cambodia border, of course, but all over the world. There are so many things we can do to help stop child trafficking. Who knew that digging a well would be one of them? Now you do. See how God shows you a problem...and then gives you a solution?

For more information: www.love146.org.

at Rebecca's home. Her dining room looked like a Victorian tea room filled with scones, pastries, and fragrant teas. Meanwhile her living room was filled with Jean's fluffy comforters piled on chairs, couches, and tables. For a donation of $50, we told the women who feasted on Rebecca's creations, they could pick out one of Jean's comforters and I would hand carry it to Thailand on my next visit and give it to the safe house that was about to welcome twelve more girls. We attached little tags to the comforters and each woman wrote out her own note to the girl who would soon be snuggled under it.

But wait, there's more. My sister Kathryn is a jewelry designer and offered to donate some of her samples. For each comforter that the women bought, they could pick out a piece of Kathryn's MetaLace jewelry to keep for themselves. It was like a "gift with purchase" and they loved it.

By the time the tea party was over, we raised more than $1,000 for Born2Fly and I had a couple of suitcases full of comforters ready to take to Thailand on my next trip. A month after I got back from delivering them, Jillian emailed me photos of the comforters on the beds in the new building, ready for the girls to arrive.

Look what God did. He took someone who had no idea why she was making comforters, someone who loved hosting tea parties, someone who made beautiful jewelry, someone who was about to get on a plane to Thailand, and someone who was about to welcome twelve girls rescued from trafficking. Who else but God could weave all that together? He took the gifts and passions

AUDACIOUS

"Life begins at the end of your comfort zone."

—Neale Donald Walsch

"In those days and at that time I will cause a righteous Branch of David to spring forth; and He shall execute justice and righteousness on the earth."

—Jeremiah 33:15 NAS

Audacious abolitionists

Tweeting for justice

This is why I love Twitter. (Please take note, people who think all we tweet about is what we ate for lunch.) A few days after the 2010 earthquake in Haiti, I saw a tweet from someone standing outside an orphanage in Haiti where traffickers were openly soliciting orphans. The person was desperately tweeting for someone to send law enforcement to stop what was happening, or media to expose it.

I knew my colleague Pat Bradley, president of International Crisis Aid, was in Haiti. Pat has rescued kids from slavery in many countries and as soon as the earthquake hit Haiti, he was there bringing supplies and help.

I retweeted the call for help to Pat and he got back to me within moments. His team was overwhelmed at another orphanage and sadly could not get to this one. Meanwhile someone else did get some international media attention on what was happening at the original orphanage—all thanks to Twitter.

Flash forward a few weeks. Pat emailed me, "Since you tweeted me regarding trafficking in Haiti, it never left my mind." He and his colleague started investigating and found a red-light district that was as bad as any they'd seen in Ethiopia—on the road that led to the very orphanage we had tweeted about. "Girls are paid $1.00 for services," Pat wrote me. "There are several hundred girls. To say these are horrible conditions is a gross understatement."

The next day Pat emailed me again: "We went back to the red-light district yesterday and gave out gift packs to about 200 girls. They told us it was the first time anyone did something nice with no strings attached. Today we returned with a group from a church in Texas. While walking around I felt God point to different girls to rescue. We are going to set them up with a roadside kiosk selling a variety of products. If they are successful it will make it possible for us to rescue others from this horrible situation."

What injustice do you see right in front of you? What injustice did you hear about that you can't get out of your mind? What solution is God giving you for it?

For more information: www.crisisaid.org.

inside them and did something to fight injustice. All those women could have said, "I can't do anything," but God took all of them and created something unique. Something audacious.

Do you think maybe He can do the same thing with you?

One night Rebecca and I drove to a city about an hour away where God seemed to be showing up every night with joy. The spiritual atmosphere was so amazing that you never knew what was going to happen from night to night, and we just couldn't get enough of it. We'd get there early so we'd be first in line to get in—I'm talking first in line of 12,000 people. That's how hungry we were for this exciting move of God. So one night while we were there, in the middle of worship God decided to download to me a script for a short video about child trafficking. It was a complete word-for-word script and I could even see the pictures—which happened to be my own photos of kids I'd taken all over the world.

Remember I said most of my pictures were average run-of-the-mill not horrible but not great—yet my pictures of kids somehow were amazing? Those were the pictures God was showing me that could make up this video, the script of which He was downloading to me in the middle of worship. I turned to Rebecca and said, "Do you think Jonathan would be interested in making a video for Born2Fly?" Jonathan was Rebecca's son, the one she and her husband, Gary, were homeschooling. One of Jonathan's passions was filmmaking and even though he was still a teenager at the time, he was getting really good at it.

"This hour in history needs a dedicated circle of transformed nonconformists. The saving of our world from pending doom will come not from the actions of a conforming majority but from the creative maladjustment of a transformed minority."

—Martin Luther King, Jr.

AUDACIOUS

"To deny people their rights before the Most High, to deprive them of justice—would not the LORD see such things?"

—Lamentations 3:35-36 NAS

What's the big idea?

Feeling disturbed?

This is a prayer attributed to explorer Sir Francis Drake who sailed around the world for England in 1577. If you're feeling audacious, pray this prayer. Warning: It's dangerous. It's audacious. You may find yourself exploring unknown realms in your own world:

> Disturb us, Lord, when we are too well pleased with ourselves, when our dreams have come true because we have dreamed too little, when we arrive safely because we have sailed too close to the shore.

> Disturb us, Lord, when with the abundance of things we possess, we have lost our thirst for the waters of life; having fallen in love with life, we have ceased to dream of eternity; and in our efforts to build a new earth, we have allowed our vision of the new Heaven to dim.

> Disturb us, Lord, to dare more boldly, to venture on wider seas where storms will show your mastery; where losing sight of land, we shall find the stars. We ask you to push back the horizons of our hopes; and to push into the future in strength, courage, hope, and love.

What thoughts come to mind as you pray this? Where is God disturbing you? In what way do you feel like you're about to sail around the world?

_____

_____

_____

A few days later I talked to Jonathan and told him what happened. "I've got the script," I said, "and I've got the photos. Would you help us make a video we could put on our website?" At the time there was almost no awareness of child trafficking and I knew a video could really help people see what was happening to these children all over the world.

Jonathan was game so I wrote out the script. I kept trying to "sanitize" it and make it less in-your-face, but God finally said to me, "That's not the script I gave you." And it wasn't. I quit trying to make child trafficking palatable and wrote out the script word-for-word that He had downloaded to me during worship. It was called "Get Angry. Please."

About a month later, Jonathan sent me what he thought was the first draft. Remember, I'm a writer and journalist so I'm used to edits and changes and dozens of drafts, and was expecting that for this project. Surprise, surprise, I not only loved what he sent me but the only changes were a couple of spelling errors in some of the text. "Do you know how amazing it is that you nailed it on the first shot?" I asked Jonathan. He just shrugged and to this day I don't think he realizes the awesomeness of what he did on the first try.

We uploaded the video to YouTube and people all over the world have since watched it. We also posted it on the Born2Fly website to get people angry enough about what's happening to these children that they'll take action.

So here we go again. God took someone who had a file full of amazing photos of kids from all over the world and downloaded a

AUDACIOUS

"If you find a path with no obstacles, it probably doesn't lead anywhere."

—Frank A. Clark

"If the wicked man turns from all his sins which he has committed and observes all My statutes and practices justice and righteousness, he shall surely live; he shall not die."

—Ezekiel 18:21 NAS

What's the big idea?

Visualize: Rehearsing success instead of rehearsing failure

"The active imagination has no trouble imagining the negative outcomes of your new plan, your next speech or that meeting you have coming up," writes one of my fav authors, Seth Godin. "It's easy to visualize and even rehearse all the things that can go wrong…When you choose to visualize the path that works, you're more likely to shore it up and create an environment where it can take place. Rehearsing failure is simply a bad habit, not a productive use of your time."*

It's easy to rehearse possible failures. In fact, we covered that in a previous "big idea." So now I want you to rehearse possible success. Get comfortable. Lie down if you want. Think about your big idea and rehearse it as a success. What would it look like? Allow yourself to be extravagant with yourself. Allow God to be extravagant with you.

What success did you visualize? _____

_____

_____

How did you feel? _____

_____

_____

_____

* Seth Godin, Rehearsing failure, rehearsing success, February 26, 2013, http://sethgodin.typepad.com/seths_blog/2013/02/rehearsing-failure-rehearsing-success.html

script to her. He took someone just out of high school who wanted to go into filmmaking. And He matched them up and created a video that told thousands of people they should get angry about the fact that kids are being raped for profit dozens of times a night. Who else but God could orchestrate that? He took the gifts and passions inside each one of us and created something to fight injustice. Jonathan could have said, "Listen, Diana, I'm not a professional. Why don't you find someone else?" but he didn't. God took his passion and created something unique. Something audacious.

Do you think maybe He can do the same thing with you?

On the other side of the planet another young filmmaker lives in Asia. I can't share her real name for reasons you'll soon see so we'll call her Stephanie. One day Stephanie was in Pattaya, Thailand, and saw young kids being openly trafficked. She got angry, all right— not just that foreigners were buying these kids right in front of her but also because no one was doing anything about it. Stephanie couldn't stop thinking about what she had seen and decided if no one else was doing anything to bring these traffickers to their knees, she would. She bought a hidden camera and microphone and on her next vacation she flew back to Pattaya. She walked up and down the beach talking with men who were openly buying little children (boys and girls) and she secretly filmed them. (You can read more about Stephanie's story later in this book—"Negotiating the sale of a three year old.")

> "Everything you believe to be impossible is."
>
> —Seth Godin

> "Again, when a wicked man turns away from his wickedness which he has committed and practices justice and righteousness, he will save his life."
>
> —Ezekiel 18:27 NAS

So now she had hours of film and she had no idea why. The months went by and I know she was frustrated and angry that kids like that little girl were still being sold night after night on the same beach where she walked. But God still didn't tell her what to do with all the footage, and all her efforts to do something with it on her own came to nothing.

Flash forward a year or so later to an anti-trafficking rally in the U.S. I spoke at the rally and afterwards a young filmmaker named Matt came up to me to talk. "I'm going to Thailand to film a documentary on child trafficking and I need some contacts," he said. "Can you help me?"

I don't give out names of contacts to just anyone, of course. Matt said he was an intern with an anti-trafficking organization that I know well, so I checked it out with the head of the organization who said Matt was indeed an intern and was working on a documentary. Green light. I shared with him some contacts on the ground in Thailand. I also told him I had a friend who had some footage he might be interested in.

Is this pattern starting to sound familiar? God took two young filmmakers on opposite sides of the world—one with undercover footage and no audience for it, and another who had the audience but needed footage. He matched them up and we're waiting to see what happens. I have no doubt it's going to be audacious. Who else but God could pull that off? He took the gifts and passions inside them and created something totally unique to stop the demand side of trafficking. Stephanie could have told Matt, "No,

"Practice justice and righteousness."

—Ezekiel 45:9 NAS

this is my footage. I'm going to wait until I can do something with it myself." Matt could have said, "I want to shoot my own footage." But they didn't. God took their passion, gifts, and skills and created something unique. Something audacious.

I want you to notice something interesting about these three stories and the people involved in them. The only one working full-time in anti-trafficking work is me. The rest of them either had jobs that had nothing to do with trafficking, or were in school. You absolutely do not need to be a professional to make a difference. Please don't let the devil or your own self-critic tell you otherwise.

Or you might be a professional and be really skilled at what you're doing. Remember my *Adventures With PawPaw* books—the ones I wrote about a little dog who travels the world introducing young children to other countries and cultures? The illustrator for those books is Leah Wiedemer and I loved her illustrations so much that I asked her to illustrate the wordless book for the Born2Fly Project to stop child trafficking. Leah took my storyline—the tale of a caterpillar named Blossom who has a dream to fly—and turned it into a wordless book with more than 500 illustrations. It's easy to illustrate "Blossom walked to school," but how in the world do you illustrate some of the lessons Blossom learned, such as "Choices have consequences"—and do it without words? Leah did, and today her illustrations are helping to reach kids before the traffickers do in more than sixty-five countries around the world.

As Leah worked on the book, she started doing her own research about what was happening in the horror-filled world of child

"Is anyone laughing at your goals? If not, think bigger."

—Anonymous

"I will betroth you to me forever; I will betroth you in righteousness and justice, in love and compassion."

—Hosea 2:19 NIV

Audacious abolitionists

501 unwanted girls

Dr. P.P. Job and his wife, Mary, adopted 501 unwanted little girls in India. They legally adopted every one of them, built homes for them, and even built schools—elementary through Ph.D.—for them to attend. Yeah, I was pretty amazed, too.

To give you an idea of the status of girls in India, this is the greeting given to a woman on her wedding day: "May you be the mother of a hundred sons." In India, almost no one wants a daughter. Every day an estimated 2,000 girls go missing in India. Every year 5 million girls are aborted in government hospitals in India—simply because they are girls.

"From abortion and infanticide," Dr. Job told me, "it goes on to denying education to the girl child, later to abuse of women. When a boy is born, there is celebration. When a girl is born, there is mourning."

The story for these 501 girls is doubly tragic. They were orphaned when their parents were murdered. Their parents were Christians and were killed for their faith. Dr. Job and his wife know something about that; their two sons were killed for their Christian faith. Michael was twenty-one and in medical school, and his older brother, John, was murdered a few years later. Dr. Job and his wife started this amazing orphanage in their honor.

In India there is no lack of demand for the insatiable child-trafficking industry, and 501 suddenly orphaned little girls would have been prime targets for recruiters. Thankfully Dr. Job and his wife took them in. Each one is one more little girl off the streets and in school. One more little girl who will not be trafficked for sex or labor.

For more information: www.mjc.ac.in.

trafficking and got particularly angry about kids forced into labor slavery. In parts of Africa, for example, kids labor for ten hours a day picking cocoa beans used to make chocolate—for pennies a day. They don't go to school; they work in dangerous conditions, and are often abused by their employers. There's almost no hope of escape for them. Think about that the next time you pop a chocolate-chip cookie into your mouth. Get angry. Please. Leah got so angry that she started a co-op, Fair Trade Mission, selling fair-trade products, including chocolate, coffee, and other products normally harvested by slave labor. She sources the products herself to make sure the companies that produce them really don't employ underage children and pay workers a fair wage for their labor. She created an online store where people can buy products that are certified free of slave labor.

Sound familiar? God took someone who loved to paint and had already illustrated three children's books, and used her to create not only a wordless children's book that's part of an anti-trafficking program reaching children in sixty-five countries, but also tapped into her passion to stop slave labor. And by the way she gives part of the profits to Born2Fly each month.

God took Leah's gifts (art) and her passion (stopping slave labor), and came up with an audacious work of art that's making a difference. Do you think He could do the same with you?

If you're still discovering God's plan for you, don't panic. The discovery process is part of your journey. Ryan Brackett is on that journey, too. He learned about trafficking in high school. He was

"Nobody succeeds beyond his or her wildest expectations unless he or she begins with some wild expectations."

—Ralph Charell

"Therefore, return to your God, Observe kindness and justice, and wait for your God continually."

—Hosea 12:6 NAS

"Somewhere in the world, someone is doing something that you decided couldn't be done."

—Seth Godin

home sick one day and happened to watch Lifetime's miniseries, Human Trafficking. Ryan was horrified by what he learned; his anger led him to do more research, which he used for a class speech.

Ryan has since graduated from university and knows God is calling him to a lifetime of anti-trafficking activism—although he doesn't yet know exactly where he will plug in. While he's searching, he's stayed busy. He has helped a number of anti-trafficking organizations either as a volunteer or intern—International Justice Mission (IMJ), Florida Abolitionist, Rapha House, and the Coalition of Immokalee Workers. In 2013 he attended IJM's Advocacy Summit in Washington DC, which was strategic because he loves the political process. He believes God is calling him to "walk alongside" some of these organizations so that he can advocate for the cause of those oppressed by and at risk for trafficking. He is also interested in influencing people to leverage their power as consumers to create more ethically sourced products. In fact one of his favorite lines is what Ashley Judd said in Call + Response: "I don't want to wear someone else's despair. I don't want to eat someone else's tragedy."

I've worked with Ryan on the Greater Orlando Human Trafficking Task Force and I've seen his passion for accuracy. He read the manuscript for *Audacious* (and yes found some stats that were not accurate—and gave me better information than I had). Ryan is still piecing together God's plan for him and although he doesn't have all the puzzle pieces yet, he knows it will involve advocacy and organizing. As Ryan continues to ask God for more details, God is, I'm sure, very happy to give them. Do you think He could do the same for you?

"They trample on the heads of the poor as on the dust of the ground and deny justice to the oppressed. Father and son use the same girl and so profane my holy name."

—Amos 2:7 NIV

Not many people went through September 11 and Hurricane Katrina, but my friend Jané Gautier Shadoin did. Jané has been involved in fashion her entire adult life as a stylist, in sales as well as entertainment/fashion event planning in the U.S. and France, where she lived for fifteen years. In 2001 she returned to the U.S. and lived in Biloxi, Mississippi, where her family is. When Katrina hit, she lost everything—home, work, possessions, and more.

That, and many other life crises, did not stop her but instead fueled her passion to do good. Jané was visiting me after one of my trips to Thailand and I showed her some of the beautiful jewelry made by girls rescued from trafficking. She held up one of the necklaces and said, "If we market this right, we could sell these here in the U.S." And that's exactly what she did. She took what she knew how to do and launched out in an entirely new direction—founding The Butterfly Project. Her line includes jewelry made by women rescued in China, Haiti, Thailand, and elsewhere.

God took someone who loved fashion, knew fashion merchandising and had survived numerous traumatic events herself. He took something broken and created something beautifully audacious out of it that is helping women and girls all over the world. Do you think He could do the same with you?

Let me tell you about Vivienne Harr. She's just eight years old. Last year she saw a photo of two child slaves in Nepal who were carrying rocks strapped across their heads. She decided to "make a stand" against it and free 500 slaves. She set up a "lemon-aid" stand in her hometown of Half Moon Bay, California, and raised more than

AUDACIOUS

"They didn't know it was impossible, so they did it."

—Mark Twain

"Hate evil, love good; establish justice in the gate."

—Amos 5:15 NKJV

"Justice, temporarily defeated, is stronger than evil triumphant."

—Martin Luther King, Jr.

$50,000, which she donated to a non-profit organization that works to stop human trafficking. Her story was featured on CBS News, Yahoo News, The Huffington Post, The BBC World News, and in media from the Netherlands to Australia. Vivienne set up a Facebook cause page (Facebook/makeastandlemonade) that quickly grew to more than 50,000 followers who not only learned about the horrors of child slave labor but what they could do about it. On 12/12/12 she set up a "lemon-aid" stand on the other side of the country—in Times Square, New York, with live coverage on Twitter, Facebook, YouTube, and Instagram.

If God can use an audacious eight-year-old girl who got angry and decided to make lemonade out of lemons, do you think He can use you? Notice that most of these people did not just raise awareness or raise funds. Most of them did something specific that fell into one of the three Ps—prevention, protection, or prosecution—either building a safe house, going after buyers, marketing jewelry to support rescued victims, etc. Also please notice that none of these people had media backing, celebrity endorsements, corporate sponsorships, grants, funding, or any of the connections you might think you need in order to make a difference in the world. They might have gotten it after they started, but they didn't start out with any of that. And you don't need to, either. All you need is the dream that God put in your heart and is trying desperately to get you to pull out.

"Let justice run down like water, and righteousness like a mighty stream."

—Amos 5:24 NKJV

Uncovering the plan that God has already put in you

ary Haugen, founder of International Justice Mission, has rescued a lot of enslaved people all over the world and he said he's never yet heard one of them ask, "Where was God?" Instead, they ask, "Where were God's people?"

Even enslaved people themselves know that God works in partnership with God's people. That's why God's people have to act. We've already seen that the injustice of child trafficking is on His heart. I personally have felt God has actually stood up from His throne, like He did when He saw Stephen about to be martyred. He's angry at this injustice. This is His *kairos* timing to end it. *Kairos* is God's timing—as opposed to *chronos,* which is human time.

Earlier we saw God's heart for justice. We already know you have a heart for justice or you wouldn't be nearly finished with a book about something you didn't care about. In this chapter we're going to melt both those hearts together—God's heart and your heart. At the same time we're going to release you to dream big dreams that dismantle injustices. Remember our promise:

"Woe to those who devise iniquity, and work out evil on their beds! At morning light they practice it, because it is in the power of their hand."

—Micah 2:1 NKJV

What's the big idea?

A fleece

Sometimes you need a sign from God to make sure you're on the right path. I totally get that. When Gideon wanted confirmation of what he thought God was telling him, he put a piece of lamb's wool on the threshing floor—a fleece. He told God if it was covered with dew in the morning, he'd know God was saying "yes" to him. The next morning there was so much dew on it that Gideon could wring it out. He wasn't convinced, however, so the next night he asked for another sign: that the ground would be wet but the fleece would be dry. The next morning that's exactly what happened.

Did God think Gideon didn't have enough faith because he asked for a sign? That he was rebellious and spiritually deaf because he asked for a second sign? Apparently not. God didn't strike him dead for asking. In fact, He not only answered him and but He also gave him even more clarification of what He wanted Gideon to do. So it's not a lack of faith to ask God to give you a sign. Just remember that Gideon didn't put out the fleece without first committing to follow through, so don't do this exercise unless you, too, will follow through.

Thinking about your big idea, what question do you need God to answer for

you? _____

What fleece can you put out for Him to answer? _____

_____

If He responds, what would He be saying to you about your idea?

_____

And how will you respond? _____

God has already put gifts and longings inside you that equip you to do this. In this chapter we're going help you specifically identify what those are. You might say we're going to go from awareness to action. Yes, I'm forcing you to. You don't want to stand before God some day and have to explain why you didn't use the talents He gave you. Why you were so incensed by the thought of children being raped for profit thirty or forty times a night but you didn't feel worthy enough or equipped enough or ready enough to act on the very plans God gave you. I know you don't want that little scenario to play out.

Hopefully you've been doing the "What's the big idea?" creativity exercises and are beginning to get a picture of your big idea to stop child trafficking. I want to ask you three questions that will help you identify that plan that God has already put inside you. First, "Who is God?" Or perhaps a more accurate question would be, "Who is your understanding of God?" If we're going to partner with the God of justice, we have to understand who it is we're partnering with. Here's one of my favorite quotes from one of my favorite books, which I've already told you about, *The Artist's Way,* by Julia Cameron. It's a quote from Michele Shea: "Creativity is…seeing something that doesn't exist already. You need to find out how you can bring it into being and that way be a playmate with God." If you don't understand that concept of being a playmate with God, if your view of God is a mean stern figure with a ruler waiting to slap your hand when you make a mistake, it's going to be really difficult for you to partner with Him.

AUDACIOUS

"The women of My people you cast out from their pleasant houses; from their children you have taken away My glory forever."

—Micah 2:9 NKJV

Audacious abolitionists

The Petticoat Project

A few years ago my brother-in-law, friend, purpose coach, and Born2Fly board member, Dr. John Stanko, turned sixty years old—and I gave him underwear to celebrate. John has been to Africa more times than I've been to the grocery store. A few years ago he was in Zimbabwe and packing to return home. He threw out a pair of "holy" underwear that had reached the end of the line. The maid found them in the trash and asked for permission to take them home to her grandchild.

Needless to say, John was deeply moved. He learned that little girls often don't go to school simply because they don't have any underwear. Girls who don't get an education are much more likely to be trafficked than girls who do. How sad that something as simple as some underwear could make such a huge difference in a little girl's life.

So John decided to take them some. He launched the Petticoat Project, started collecting underwear for girls, and he and a team delivered everything in person to an orphanage in Kenya. He brought more than 2,500 pairs in one trip alone (along with thousands of children's books, part of the work of his Deborah Foundation, which establishes children's libraries and learning centers in Africa). It's made a huge difference in the lives of many girls. So for John's sixtieth birthday, I donated underwear in his name to the Petticoat Project. Now if God can get creative with underwear, what is He telling you?

For more information: www.stankomondaymemo.com/2013/04/600-underwear-for-my-birthday.html.

Imagine if you were in business with someone. Wouldn't you want it to be someone you could trust, hang out with and talk with over a cup of coffee, and feel free enough to shoot out some ideas and not feel threatened or rejected or intimidated? You're about to go into business with God as your partner so ask Him to show you who He really is. You cannot partner with Him to tear down injustice if you have the wrong picture of Him—because you're not partnering with Him but with whom you think He is. And why in the world would you want to free someone from bondage, and then introduce them to *that* concept of who God is—just another form of bondage? If you need to reread about how God partnered with Esther, please do that now.

Second question: "Who are you?" A more accurate question might be, "Who is your understanding of you?" Maybe you don't feel worthy to partner with the God of the universe. Oh please. We've already seen that is false humility. If God thinks you're worthy enough, you must believe you are. Once again I remind you of that little scenario of you standing before the God of the universe trying to explain why you didn't act on the brilliant plans He's about to give you—simply because you didn't feel worthy enough. When do you think you will feel worthy? Is there a specific date? If you don't feel worthy now, trust me, you'll never feel worthy. A string of degrees after your name or a thousand classes are not going to make you worthy. He made you worthy. Already.

Third question: "What is your dream?" You may say, "I don't know," but I suspect you do. I suspect you already have some big clues about what that dream is. But it scares you so much that you think,

"It's not too late, just later than it was."

—Seth Godin

113

AUDACIOUS

"He has told you, O man, what is good; and what does the LORD require of you but to do justice, to love kindness, and to walk humbly with your God?"

—Micah 6:8 NAS

What's the big idea?

Your action steps

By the time you finish this book, I want you to have a rough idea about your big idea—and already be working on it. So you need a plan. Plans aren't always neat and pretty and organized—certainly not at the beginning. You've got to start somewhere. Start by listing five things you could maybe possibly do to move your idea forward. You don't have to do them right now (or ever). Just brainstorm five things. Don't let the self-critic edit them for you. Just brainstorm.

1 _____

2 _____

3 _____

4 _____

5 _____

Okay, now add five more:

6 _____

7 _____

8 _____

9 _____

10 _____

How did that make you feel? Put a star by the ideas that seem to have some merit. Draw a circle around the one you could work on right now. Underline the ones you'll do after that. To the right of each one you circled and underlined, write the name of someone who could help you—either from your Dream Team or someone else.

"That can't possibly be God." Oh yes it is. Bill Bright, founder of Cru, said, "If your dreams don't scare you, they're not big enough." I give you permission to dream big dreams. More importantly, God gives you permission to do that. He wants you to. In fact, He requires you to. I can't tell you what your dream is but you can, and God can. And He is.

You will probably not have a completely accurate picture of the dream inside you right now, or even by the time you finish reading this book. But that's okay. This is an ongoing process and this is just to get you started. In fact, that's why there are so many blank lines in some of the "big idea" creativity exercises; keep adding to them as you read this book. If you position yourself to pull your God idea out of you, the God who put it in there in the first place will be faithful to help you.

Did I know on day one what I was doing? No. My favorite line was, "I'm making it up as I go along." You will be, too. And people will think you're crazy, but that's all right. God thinks you're wonderful, and that's all right. He doesn't call the equipped; He equips the called.

If you're called (and you are), then you're equipped. Keep pressing in, but don't wait too long. And for God's sake don't wait until you have all the answers. Remember that perfectionism thing. And remember the "s" in audacious: "Stop preparing and start doing."

One final note: This chapter needs to come with a warning about what happens when you not only dream but make a conscious decision to move from idea to action. The dream thieves show up.

"If opportunity doesn't knock, build a door."

—Milton Berle

115

AUDACIOUS

"The Lord…is righteous; he does no wrong. Morning by morning he dispenses his justice, and every new day he does not fail, yet the unrighteous know no shame."

—Zephaniah 3:5 NIV

Audacious abolitionists

Beauty for ashes

I call Julie Taylor Shematz my "fellow red-headed abolitionist." Like me, she has red hair. Unlike me, she knows about the horrors of human trafficking firsthand because she was trafficked herself. She grew up fatherless and suffered sexual and domestic abuse, rejection, abandonment, depression, addictions, and eventually human trafficking—but God rescued her and restored her. In 2005 she launched a ministry called Beauty for Ashes to reach and restore women and children caught in the sex industry (www.beautyfromashes.org).

Julie is a perfect testimony of the premise of this book: God will show you a need (and in her case, she was right there as part of the need and broke free from it) and then show you the answer He's already put inside you. Julie took everything she knows and loves and made it part of her very effective ministry. She's an artist, so she includes art therapy in her work with rescued victims. She loves horses, so she includes equine therapy. She even went back to graduate school for a Masters of Art degree in clinical mental health counseling so that she can offer equine psychotherapy—free of charge to victims. She knows the sex industry more than most, so she wrote a best-practices, faith-based curriculum for sex industry outreach and aftercare.

What do you know more than most—possibly even through tragedy—that God can use to help stop child trafficking?

For more information: www.beautyfromashes.org

You are challenging the status quo and everything will come against you to push you back into your nice neat life. You'll meet resistance every single day. Ask me how I know. There were days I wanted to quit. In fact, there were entire seasons when I convinced myself that my role in B2F was over and it was time to turn it over to someone else. That's the "c" in "audacious": counterattack. You are confronting one of the most heinous forms of evil on the planet, so why wouldn't you encounter a little resistance? Of course you will. But remember you're in a business partnership and your partner—God Himself—will be right there to fight on your behalf. It helps, by the way, to have some human partners, too. That's your Dream Team.

And speaking of dreams, let's end with this:

> "With every dream, every vision, and every promised land there is a challenge and call to overcome. The coat of many colors that was given to Joseph is a picture of what God gives to us to put on (see Genesis 37:3). God is a God of color, of diversity, of beauty, and of brightness. He takes us beyond the place of grey and dullness, calling us to dream beyond ourselves into a place that overflows and affects others.
>
> "Just as Joseph had the dream that God had given him, he also had to overcome many things to see those dreams come to pass. In a moment he inherited a kingdom. When the fullness of time comes for our dreams, God is faithful to see that they come to pass. Our faithfulness, commitment, and uncompromising heart [are] required

> "Greatness is not a function of circumstance. Greatness is largely a matter of conscious choice and discipline."
>
> —Jim Collins

"This is what the LORD Almighty said: 'Administer true justice; show mercy and compassion to one another.'"

—Zechariah 7:9 NIV

"If your dreams don't scare you, they're not big enough."

—Bill Bright

to inherit the fullness of what God has for each of us. In order to inherit a promise, we must have a dream with the accompanying grace to overcome in the seasons of life that are packaged with these dreams.""

What about _____ [fill in your name]?

Here's what I don't want to happen right now. I don't want you to get to the last page of this book and say, "Wow, that Diana is totally brilliant and inspiring," close the book, and go back to life as usual, being angry about child trafficking but not really doing anything to stop it. That's why in these final pages I want to push you out of your comfort zone so that you can start acting on all the things God has been speaking to you as you've been reading the chapters and doing the "What's the big idea?" exercises. It's one thing to be inspired. It's another to take action. "I fear that we're more in love with the idea of changing the world than changing the world," warned Eugene Cho, one of the founders of the Justice Conference. Don't let that happen to you.

Remember our promise: The God of justice has already put creative solutions inside you to help end the injustice that you see. My goal is to help you take everything you've been learning, sensing, hearing, and feeling in the previous chapters and now step out in faith and start to take action. "But I don't know where I'm going," you may say. "I've just got some vague random ideas—what do I do first? And anyway I'm not ready."

---

* John Belt, Elijah List, January 4, 2013

"He will proclaim justice to the nations...A bruised reed he will not break, and a smoldering wick he will not snuff out, till he has brought justice through to victory."

—Matthew 12:18-20 NIV

Who does that sound like? Yup, the self-critic. At this point in the book the self-critic will have the volume turned up to ten. He'll be screaming at you and telling you you're not ready, you need to wait, you need a degree, you need to read one more book, wait one more week, one more month, one more year. He is audacious. And you must be even more audacious if you're ever going to do anything. You have to make a concerted effort right now not to listen to him. His job is to keep talking and your job is not to listen to him or agree with him. Please make this commitment right now:

I will not listen to the self-critic. I will not agree with him. I will recognize when he's talking to me and I will ignore him.

Signed: _____

Date: _____

Trafficked children have a price on their heads—and you have a price on you, too. It will cost you a lot to go after this audacious dream—possibly everything. And I'm not talking necessarily about money. How much are you willing to pay? Are you willing to be misunderstood, unappreciated, called weird, unrealistic, with your head in the clouds? "Why don't you get a job? A real job? A nice nine-to-five job?"

"Will not God bring about justice for His elect who cry to Him day and night, and will He delay long over them? I tell you that He will bring about justice for them quickly."

—Luke 18:7-8 NAS

What's the big idea?

Your ladder

Draw a ladder here:

At the top of the ladder, write a word or draw a picture to symbolize your big idea that God has been downloading to you about how you can help stop child trafficking. In the last big idea exercise, you brainstormed some of the things you could do to move that big idea forward. Let's turn those into specific steps. Which is the main one you circled? Write it on the lower rung of your ladder. On the next rungs, list the other steps you listed. Put them in the best order you know right now. This order will change so don't worry that it's not perfect.

To the side of the ladder draw a person who can be a coach or encourager to help you at each rung by providing motivation and commitment when you face impatience or discouragement. This is probably someone on your Dream Team—an friend, a trusted friend of the family, an older family member, a mentor, or someone who has had the same goal in the past and achieved it.

Review this ladder regularly and update the steps, checking off those you've achieved.

It's going to take work, sacrifice, and giving up something else so that you can do this. Activism is called that because it's active. You will never do anything by being passive. If you want to just keep being aware, then please just go like a few more Facebook pages. If you want to make a difference, if you want to be audacious, you have to get off the couch. Audacious people stay up late and labor over their dreams while others just dream. Audacious people are thermostats not thermometers. Audacious people pay with their blood, sweat, and tears to make their dream a reality.

You will never, ever have all the puzzle pieces in place before you start, so what are you waiting for? Act on the idea God gave you. Take a first step today. He'll show you step two after you take step one, not before. And He *will* show you, I promise you. It takes faith to take action. It doesn't take any faith to sit on your couch dreaming about your idea for the next year.

> "A year from now you may wish you had started today."
>
> —Anonymous

> "If you really want to do something, you'll find a way. If you don't, you'll find an excuse."
>
> —Anonymous

Children who are being raped for profit thirty times a night cannot wait for your idea to be perfect. They need you now. I can give you only so much motivation, direction, and encouragement. Ultimately it's up to you to hang out with the God of justice and let Him download His custom-made-for-you idea, just like He did for me. If

AUDACIOUS

"You have to have an idea of what you are going to do, but it should be a vague idea."

—Pablo Picasso

"He [is] just and the justifier."

—Romans 3:26 NKJV

What's the big idea?

Audaciousness

Make a poster to remind yourself to be audacious. Do it on paper, on your computer, as an Instagram—whatever you like. You can use these words or your own or one of the quotes you've read throughout this book:

"Audacious people dream audaciously and do audacious things to dismantle audacious injustices."

"Traffickers think audaciously so I need to, too."

"If traffickers are a ten at audacious, I need to be an eleven."

"I will train myself to think audaciously. Everything in me and around me will try to keep me from this, but I commit to being audacious in my quest to stop child trafficking."

He did it for me and all the other people you've read about in this book, why in the world wouldn't He do it for you?

Go be audacious.

"But about the Son he says, 'Your throne, O God, will last for ever and ever; a scepter of justice will be the scepter of your kingdom.'"

—Hebrews 1:8 NIV

\#

By the numbers

12 things child traffickers don't want you to know

1 Child traffickers have recruiters in your schools in the U.S.

2 Recruiters are other kids.

3 Child traffickers monitor Facebook, Flickr, and other social media sites looking for vulnerable kids.

4 They work in malls all over the U.S., including in your city.

5 There's money to be made buying and selling children. You can sell a bag of drugs once but you can sell a child over and over again.

6 Human trafficking is organized crime. It's the second most lucrative illegal industry on the planet after illegal drugs.

7 These are not "bad" kids, just vulnerable ones.

8 Most kids are rescued because someone saw something that didn't look right and knew where to call.

9 Warning signs you can look for

10 What to ask if you think someone is being trafficked

11 Your city probably already has an anti-trafficking task force.

12 There's plenty of information on the web to keep you aware and help you protect yourself and your children.

Don't tell the traffickers, but you can find all the information they don't want you to know; it's throughout this book.

73 ways to tell if someone is being trafficked

Some slaves are kept out of the public eye. Others are right in front of you—waitresses, nail salon workers, kids in your neighborhood, laborers you see every day. I'm talking about actual slaves. Here are dozens of ways to tell if someone might be trafficked; just one of them, of course, doesn't mean someone is being trafficked, but string enough of them together and you can say, "If something doesn't look right, it probably isn't." I use feminine pronouns in this list, but victims can also be boys. For child trafficking these indicators primarily refer to tweens and teenagers.

General behavior

1   Sudden, unexplained changes in any of these areas.

2   Change in wardrobe; for example, used to wear inexpensive normal clothes but now wears more revealing clothes, or expensive clothes.

3   Suddenly has clothes, jewelry, and accessories that are way beyond her age and income, especially if she doesn't have a job.

4   Change in the music she listens to; for example, she used to like Taylor Swift and Selena Gomez but is now into Snoop, 50 Cent, Lil' Jon, and music with graphic lyrics.

5   You can never speak with her alone.

6   Answers appear to be scripted and rehearsed.

7   Frequently changes stories; inconsistent.

8   Has few or no personal possessions.

9 Has very little or no pocket money.

10 Not in control of his/her own money; no financial records or bank account; someone else (trafficker or pimp) controls it.

11 Not in control of her own identification documents (ID or passport); someone else controls it.

12 Has false ID.

13 Possesses hotel or motel room keys, key cards, business cards, matchbooks, etc.

14 Has more than one cell phone.

15 Not allowed or able to speak for herself; someone else insists on being present (and translating if she's from another country).

16 Unexplained absences from school (yes, victims can still be in school while being trafficked).

Physical

17 Signs of physical abuse including unexplained bruises, scratches, cuts, broken bones, physical restraint, confinement, rape, or torture, or untreated medical problems.

18 Has new tattoos or burns, perhaps with her new boyfriend's name on it, indicating branding or ownership.

19 Is always exhausted.

20 Has calluses on her feet.

21 Lacks health care.

22 Appears malnourished.

23 When taken to a doctor, hospital or clinic for treatment, is kept under surveillance; trafficker may act as a translator.

24 Has signs of malnutrition, dehydration or poor personal hygiene.

25 Has sexually transmitted diseases and infections.

26 Has critical illnesses including diabetes, cancer or heart disease that are untreated.

27 Recurrent pregnancy tests; numerous pregnancies and abortions; unsure who the father is.

Mental and emotional

28 Depressed, fearful, anxious, overly submissive, tense, nervous, silent, sad, and/or paranoid (any combination of these).

29 Physically or verbally abusive when you start asking questions.

30 Unusually fearful when you mention law enforcement.

31 Avoids eye contact.

32 Lack of knowledge of whereabouts and/or does not know what city she is in.

33 Loss of sense of time.

34 Numerous inconsistencies in her story.

35 Post-traumatic stress or psychological disorders.

36 Signs of verbal or psychological abuse; seems intimidated, degraded, and frightened.

37 Lies about age.

38 Disappears for long periods; frequently runs away.

39 Drug or alcohol abuse.

40 Suicide attempts.

41 Talks about sex a lot and has more knowledge than others her age.

42 Lack of regard or appropriate behavior when talking about sex; speaks explicitly about it and beyond her age level.

Friends and acquaintances

43 Brags about her new, older boyfriend (often ten years older).

44 Refers to her boyfriend as "daddy" or with other inappropriate parental terms.

45 Doesn't want to date boys her age anymore because they're too young; suddenly is more interested in men older than she is.

46 Doesn't want to be your friend anymore.

47 Doesn't want to participate in the extracurricular activities she used to enjoy.

48 Obsessed with appearance; always has her hair and nails done yet doesn't have money to pay for it. Brags that her boyfriend takes care of it for her.

49 Uses terms like "wifey," "daddy," "the family," "the game," or other terminology of the sex industry.

50 Accompanied by a controlling person or boss; doesn't speak on her own behalf.

51 Someone else has control of her personal schedule, money, I.D., travel documents.

Living conditions

52 Claims she's just visiting, can't clarify where she is staying or tell you her address.

53 Poor living conditions.

54 Lives with employer.

55 Lives with multiple people in cramped space.

56 Lives at the same premises as the brothel or work.

57 Is driven between quarters and work by a guard.

58 Bars on windows and doors.

59 Numerous cars coming and going in driveway.

60 Moves frequently, even every week.

Working conditions

61 Transported to or from work by guard.

62 Prohibited from leaving work site as she wishes.

63 Work site may look like a guarded compound from the outside.

64 High foot traffic; often many men arriving and leaving the premises.

65 High security measures such as opaque windows, boarded up windows, bars on windows, barbed wire, security cameras, locked doors, isolated location, electronic surveillance, etc; this can apply to living conditions also.

66 Owes a large debt to employer or crew leaders and is unable to pay it off or leave work until it is paid off.

67 Unpaid, paid very little, or paid only through tips.

68 Under eighteen and providing commercial sex acts.

69 Has a pimp/manager.

70 Works excessively long and/or unusual hours.

71 Is not allowed breaks or has unusual restrictions at work.

72 Was recruited through false promises concerning nature and conditions of her work.

73 Never seen leaving the premises unless escorted.*

---

* Sources: U.S. Department of Health and Human Services, U.S. Department of State, Polaris Project, HumanTrafficking.org, Opening Doors, International Institute for Abuse Counseling, Born2Fly Project

16 things to ask if you think someone is being trafficked

Here are questions to ask if you suspect someone is being trafficked. (Most of these apply to tweens, teens, and young adults, not young children.) Keep in mind that victims are brainwashed and traumatized; they will protect their traffickers so you will probably not get straight or truthful answers to these questions, but you can always ask. Make your conversation just that—a conversation. Don't act like you're interrogating her or she'll run. Don't ask all these questions or she'll know you suspect something. Victims are taught that the only ones they can trust are their captors.

If you believe you've found a victim, do not try to rescue her yourself. Child trafficking is organized crime and you will be putting her life and yours in danger. Instead call 911 or the National Human Trafficking hotline: 888-3737-888.

1   What type of work do you do?

2   Are you getting paid?

3   Is anything taken out of your pay?

4   Can you leave your job if you want to?

5   Can you come and go as you please? Are you afraid to leave? Why?

6   Have you been hurt or threatened if you tried to leave?

7   Has your family been threatened if you try to leave?

8   What are your working and living conditions like? How are you treated?

9   Do you have to ask permission to eat, sleep, or go to the bathroom?

10   Are there locks on your doors and windows so you can't get out?

11   Do you have your passport, driver's license, or identification? Who has it?

12   Has someone taken it away from you?

13   Do you live with your employer?

14   Where do you sleep and eat?

15   Are you in debt to your employer?

16   How did you arrive in this country (if she's not a U.S. citizen)?*

---

* Sources: U.S. State Department, Polaris Project, U.S. Department of Justice, Born2Fly Project

5 things you (and your little brother) can stop doing on social media right now

1   Watch what you post on social media including Facebook, Twitter, Instagram, Tagged, MySpace, DateHookup, and other sites. Traffickers regularly use social networks to recruit victims. They use the same old tricks on new platforms. Lies are lies. Just because you have a personal account on Facebook, it is not secure, it's not private, and it's certainly not closed to traffickers. Anyone can easily get on any page if they know what to do. Facebook does have strong anti-trafficking rules, but traffickers regularly get around them.

2   Don't post any picture you don't want spread around the internet. Traffickers can easily take your face and Photoshop it onto someone else's body (a body not wearing any clothes), and start selling it as porn. And definitely don't post or text any explicit pictures of yourself. Once you hit the send button, the picture is out of your control. This has happened to many teens who are helpless to stop their damaging photos—and the damage to their lives. One boy was so despondent that he committed suicide.

3   Don't accept friend requests from people you don't know. Why in the world would you friend a stranger just to appear to be popular? This is a key way traffickers lure victims. "But I'm not chatting with a trafficker," you might protest. "I'm talking to a girl my age in another state." Oh really? That "girl" could really be a thirty-year-old man who's looking for teens to traffic. It happens all the time. This happens to boys as well as girls.

4   Be careful what you say, especially unloading all your angst for the world to read. According to Jack Bennett, the FBI's cybercrimes chief in San Francisco, pimps "start looking for the cracks where they can fill the holes, whether it be a father figure or a boyfriend." And remember that your delete key doesn't work on anything you've already posted online; it's there forever.

5   If you're a parent, monitor your kids' social media profiles and activity. It's no longer an excuse to say, "I can barely operate a toaster, never mind Facebook." Learn.

8 mindsets of a trafficking victim

You're probably reading this in a nice warm room, a comfy chair at Starbucks, or somewhere else that we could describe as normal. Normal for you is what you're used to. The only way that trafficking victims can endure what they're going through is to convince themselves it's normal. The lies that traffickers tell them become the truth. Trauma, abuse, control, torture, not to mention rape for profit night after night have so messed with their brains and emotions that their normal has been redefined. That may be difficult for you to understand, but if you want to fight child trafficking, you have to understand the mindset of victim:

1. Victims are told that traffickers are their daddies. They're now part of a new "family" that loves them and cares for them. Only the traffickers have their best interests at heart, they're told; everyone else is against them, particularly law enforcement.

2. Traffickers lie to victims and threaten their families. "If you try to run, I'll kill your mother. Or your little sister."

3. In many cases victims are told that the money they earn is being sent to help their families back home. This is particularly prevalent in Asia. Needless to say, the families don't see a penny.

4. Many victims are constantly drugged, further messing up their minds. Add to that continuous inhumane treatment and nightmare conditions, physical and mental abuse, threats (often carried out), forced abortions, and more.

5. Often victims don't know what city, state, or even country they're in because they're moved around so often.

6. Many victims are from other countries. They don't speak the local language and don't understand the local culture. They may come

from countries where police are feared so they'd never think to run for help.

7 If they're brought across international borders illegally, they have no papers so even if they run away, where would they go? They have no cell phone, no money, no ID, no one to call.

8 Many victims do not even realize they're victims.

For them this is the new normal. They've redefined it. They had to in order to keep from going insane.*

---

* The new normal: The mindset of a trafficking victim, author's blog, April 2, 2013, www.dianascimone.com

18 lies that traffickers tell

1. "I can show you how to get a job as a waitress, model, or nanny."

2. "You have beautiful eyes/hair/body."

3. "You should be a model/make-up artist/on TV/in commercials."

4. "You are more mature/sophisticated than other girls your age."

5. "I have money to educate you in the city."

6. "I can help you get a visa."

7. "You'll help your family by doing what I say."

8. "I have lots of money and I want to give some to you."

9. "The money you earn will go to your family/your child."

10. "Your friends have money and nice things; why shouldn't you?"

11. "You help me and I'll help you. You can trust me."

12. "You're having sex anyway; you should charge for it."

13. "You can make some money carrying drugs or selling goods."

14. "Help me cash this check and I'll give part of it to you."

15. "You can stay with me for awhile and I'll pay for your food and clothes."

16. "Just help me out this one time."

17. "Just have sex with my friend once."

18. "I love you."*

AUDACIOUS

---

* Source: "Trafficking Safety Information for Mothers in a Nutshell." Human trafficking lecture series pilot for incarcerated women, Columbus, Ohio, 2013

4 steps to take if you think someone is being trafficked

1 First, don't try to rescue a victim unless it's absolutely necessary and you have no other options. Traffickers are ruthless and members of organized syndicates. You may put your life in danger, not to mention the victim.

2 If you're in the U.S.: Call the National Human Trafficking hotline at 888-3737-888. They may also ask you to call 911. The U.S. Department of Justice also has a hotline where you can report suspected instances of human trafficking or worker exploitation: 888-428-7581 (weekdays 9:00 a.m. to 5:00 p.m. ET). The hotline offers translation in many languages as well as TTY. After business hours, there's a message service in English, Spanish, Russian, and Mandarin.

3 If you're traveling to another country: Take this link with you. It has the global trafficking hotlines for many countries: www.state.gov/j/tip/rls/other/2011/168859.htm.

4 If you identify someone who has escaped trafficking and needs help: Many organizations provide specialized immediate assistance and aftercare that trafficking victims need such as shelter, medical care, legal assistance, foreign language translation, and other critical services. Call the National Human Trafficking hotline at 888-3737-888 for referrals in your area.

1 great principle:
"Sometimes we must interfere"

Elie Wiesel is a Holocaust survivor. He endured Auschwitz and Buchenwald concentration camps as a teenager with his father. Decades later he was awarded the Nobel Peace Prize. As you read the words of his acceptance speech—a conversation between a child and his father—think how they apply to the atrocity of child trafficking.

"[The boy] asked his father: 'Can this be true? This is the twentieth century, not the Middle Ages. Who would allow such crimes to be committed? How could the world remain silent?'

"And now the boy is turning to me. 'Tell me,' he asks, 'what have you done with my future, what have you done with your life?' And I tell him that I have tried. That I have tried to keep memory alive, that I have tried to fight those who would forget. Because if we forget, we are guilty, we are accomplices.

"And then I explain to him how naïve we were, that the world did know and remained silent. And that is why I swore never to be silent whenever wherever human beings endure suffering and humiliation. We must take sides. Neutrality helps the oppressor, never the victim. Silence encourages the tormentor, never the tormented.

"Sometimes we must interfere. When human lives are endangered, when human dignity is in jeopardy, national borders and sensitivities become irrelevant. Wherever men and women are persecuted because of their race, religion, or political views, that place must—at that moment—become the center of the universe…

"What all these victims need above all is to know that they are not alone; that we are not forgetting them, that when their voices are stifled we shall lend them ours, that while their freedom depends on ours, the quality of our freedom depends on theirs…

"We know that every moment is a moment of grace, every hour an offering; not to share them would mean to betray them. Our lives no longer belong to us alone; they belong to all those who need us desperately."*

Sometimes we must interfere. Child trafficking is a very good place to do that.

---

* Elie Wiesel, Nobel Prize acceptance speech, Oslo, Norway, December 10, 1986

18 myths about child trafficking

1   Trafficked persons are from other countries—usually illegally.
    Reality: The federal definition of human trafficking includes both U.S. citizens and foreign nationals. Both are equally protected under the federal trafficking statutes. Human trafficking encompasses transnational trafficking that crosses borders, as well as domestic or internal trafficking within a country.

2   Trafficking must involve some form of travel, transportation, or movement across state or national borders.
    Reality: The legal definition of trafficking does not require transportation, although transportation may be involved in the crime. It is more accurately described as "compelled service" where an individual's will is overborne through force, fraud, or coercion. (Force, fraud, and coercion do not have to be present for minors to be identified as trafficking victims, however.)

3   Human trafficking is another word for human smuggling.
    Reality: They are not the same. Both are entirely separate federal crimes in the U.S. Smuggling is a crime against a country's borders while human trafficking is a crime against a person. While smuggling requires illegal border crossing, human trafficking involves commercial sex acts or labor or services that are induced through force, fraud, or coercion whether or not transportation occurs. (Force, fraud, and coercion do not have to be present for minors to be identified as trafficking victims, however.)

4   Trafficking always involves physical restraint, physical force, or physical bondage.
    Reality: The legal definition of trafficking in the U.S. does not require physical restraint, bodily harm, or physical force.

Psychological means of control, such as threats, or abuse of the legal process, are sufficient elements of the crime.

5 Victims of trafficking will immediately ask for help or assistance and will self-identify as a victim of a crime.

    Reality: Victims of trafficking often do not immediately seek help or self-identify as victims of a crime due to lack of trust, self-blame, or training by the traffickers.

6 Trafficking victims always come from situations of poverty or from small rural villages.

    Reality: Although poverty is highly correlated with human trafficking because it is often an indicator of vulnerability, poverty alone is not a single factor or indicator of a human trafficking victim. Trafficking victims can come from a range of income levels and many may come from families with higher socioeconomic status.

7 Sex trafficking is the only form of human trafficking.

    Reality: Human trafficking encompasses sex trafficking, labor trafficking, and organ trafficking. It can affect men and women, children and adults, and even infants.

8 Human trafficking occurs only in illegal underground industries.

    Reality: Elements of human trafficking can be identified whenever the means of force, fraud, or coercion induce a person to perform commercial sex acts, or labor or services. (Force, fraud, and coercion do not have to be present for minors to be identified as trafficking victims, however.) Trafficking can occur in legal and legitimate business settings as well as underground markets.

9 If the trafficked person consented to be in their initial situation or was informed about what type of labor they would be doing

or that commercial sex would be involved, then it cannot be trafficking or against their will because they "knew better."

Reality: A victim cannot consent to be in a situation of human trafficking. Initial consent to commercial sex or a labor setting prior to acts of force, fraud, or coercion (or if the victim is a minor in a sex trafficking situation) is not relevant to the crime, nor is payment.

10 Foreign national trafficking victims are always undocumented immigrants or in the country illegally.

Reality: Foreign national trafficked persons can be in any country through either legal or illegal means. Although some foreign national victims are undocumented, a significant percentage may have legitimate visas for various purposes. Not all foreign national victims are undocumented.[*]

11 Women in prostitution or pornography are there because they want to be. They can leave at any time.

Reality: Some women have chosen that path, but the majority have not. They were coerced into it under false pretenses, and they are controlled and cannot leave.

12 Children in prostitution or pornography can leave at any time.

Reality: No child in prostitution or pornography is there because she chose it; someone made the decision for her and she is there by force.

13 She's not being trafficked; she's just _____. (Fill in the blank.)

Reality: "Trafficking victims may be mislabeled as victims of sexual abuse, rape, or domestic violence. Though these crimes

* Myths 1-10 excerpted from Common Myths and Misconceptions, Polaris Project National Human Trafficking Resource Center, www.polarisproject.org/human-trafficking/overview/myths-and-misconceptions

are a part of a trafficking situation, they do not encompass the extent and complexity of the exploitation that has occurred in sex trafficking. When mislabeled, victims do not receive the entire range of services or victim rights that are necessary for restoration. Further, perpetrators are not held accountable to the fullest extent of the law."*

14 Pornography has nothing to do with trafficking. Everyone should be free to look at what they want.

Reality: This has nothing to do with "freedom." Children who are in pornographic photos or films are trafficked; they were not free to choose to be in it. If you buy, sell, or look at child pornography, you are participating in child trafficking. You are committing a crime. This has nothing to do with freedom.

15 Trafficking doesn't happen here.

Reality: "Approaching human trafficking as a crime that occurs only in far off places ignores situations of forced labor or sex trafficking that may be happening closer to home. Human trafficking is not a problem that involves only foreigners or migrants, but one faced in nearly every corner of the world involving citizens who may be exploited without ever leaving their hometown."

16 She's a criminal.

Reality: "Many victims of trafficking first come to the attention of authorities due to an arrest for immigration violations, prostitution, or petty theft. Screening vulnerable populations— even if first encountered as potential defendants—for signs of force, fraud, or coercion used against them is imperative to identify human trafficking properly, to ensure that victims are not

---

* Shared Hope International, The National Report on Domestic Minor Sex Trafficking: America's Prostituted Children

punished for acts committed as a result of being subjected to trafficking, and to effectively prevent victims from being returned to an exploitive situation."

17 It's a cultural thing.

Reality: "Holding a person in servitude is not a cultural practice; it is a crime. Some victims are subjected to trafficking by members of their own family or ethnic group. Misperceptions that this is a shared value among an ethnic group ignore the methods of force and coercion used by individual traffickers, and can create a zone of impunity in an ethnic community, with the result that victims in that group will never see their abusers brought to justice."

18 Trafficking doesn't happen where prostitution is legal.

Reality: "The occurrence of trafficking does not depend on the legality of prostitution; it exists whether prostitution is legal, illegal, or decriminalized."*

* Myths 15-18 excerpted from 2013 Trafficking in Persons Report, U.S. Department of State

55 things you can do to stop child trafficking

1 Join the fight against trafficking in your own city. (Yes, it's happening there.)

2 Google the name of your city and "human trafficking" or "child trafficking." Read, learn, get angry.

3 Meet with other abolitionists in your city. If there's not a group, start one.

4 Understand the mindset of a trafficking victim. http://dianascimone.typepad.com/diana_scimone/2013/04/the-new-nomal-the-mindset-of-a-trafficking-victim.html

5 Download info for health care providers, social service agencies, and law enforcement officials. www.acf.hhs.gov/programs/orr/resource/rescue-restore-campaign-tool-kits#health

6 Pick a factsheet and learn about some aspect of human trafficking. www.state.gov/j/tip/rls/fs/index.htm

7 Order free anti-trafficking brochures, posters, info cards (in many languages). http://archive.acf.hhs.gov/trafficking/about/form.htm

8 Study how to combat trafficking of women and children; look at the links throughout this book.

9 Read about anti-trafficking legislation in the U.S. www.state.gov/g/tip/laws

10 Find out what human trafficking is and isn't.

11   Watch U.S. Immigration and Customs Enforcement awareness videos. www.ice.gov/human-trafficking/psa.htm

12   Learn what to ask if you think someone is trafficked.

13   Call the National Human Trafficking hotline to report a trafficking victim: 888-3737-888.

14   Choose a country (the one already on your heart) and learn about trafficking there.

15   Read the latest country-by-country Trafficking in Persons Report: www.state.gov/g/tip

16   Subscribe to blogs and updates from anti-trafficking groups.

17   Give a gift card to your local anti-trafficking task force to help rescued victims—grocery stores, Wal-Mart, etc.

18   Open your eyes. There's trafficking all around you.

19   Introduce Born2Fly to a foundation or corporation.

20   Host a party and make anti-trafficking t-shirts to wear. Come up with creative sayings and designs.

21   Volunteer as an intern at your local anti-trafficking task force.

22   Visit http://slavery.alltop.com. Pick a blog a day to read and leave an encouraging comment.

23   Make a Born2Fly patch or pin to wear on your backpack to spark conversation.

24   Give a gift in someone's honor. Donate to an anti-trafficking organization in his or her name.

25 Post anti-trafficking videos like "Get Angry. Please." on your Facebook page. It's at www.born2fly.org and on YouTube.

26 Download the Born2Fly anti-trafficking curriculum and teach it at your school.

27 Post instances of trafficking on www.slaverymap.org.

28 Sponsor a B2F day at your school.

29 Ask your legislators what they're doing to stop the traffic—or if they even know it's happening in their district or state.

30 Write a letter to the editor of your school paper or favorite online news source.

31 Donate to anti-trafficking organizations such as B2F.

32 Make and display your own anti-trafficking posters in schools, offices, and churches.

33 Blog, tweet, and Facebook about child trafficking.

34 Pray and ask God to open your eyes to see what's happening around you.

35 Learn about trafficking in countries where you travel.

36 Flex your political muscles. Find out about anti-trafficking laws in your state and work to strengthen them.

37 Forgo birthday presents. Instead ask family and friends to donate to B2F in your name.

38 Take a voluntourism trip to help anti-trafficking efforts.

39 Pick a country and take an immersion trip.

40 Start an anti-trafficking book club. Read and discuss *Audacious*, *Terrify No More*, *Good News About Injustice*, *Priceless*, and other books.

41 Organize a fund-raising party for Born2Fly.

42 Host a house meeting or dorm meeting. Watch *China's Stolen Children* or *Nefarious*.

43 Read about modern-day abolitionists.

44 Set up Google alerts for "child trafficking," "slavery," etc.

45 Learn which products are fair-trade so you're not supporting child slave labor.

46 Study the red flags that may indicate human trafficking.

47 Learn questions that you can ask a potential victim.

48 Discover your Slavery Footprint (www.slaveryfootprint.org; note it is not entirely accurate).

49 Know what's in your supply chain by reading the U.S. Department of Labor's List of Goods Produced by Child Labor or Forced Labor. www.dol.gov/ilab/programs/ocft/PDF/2011TVPRA.pdf

50 Petition companies you do business with and ask them to look for and remove forced labor in their supply lines. www.chainstorereaction.com

51 Offer your help to your local anti-trafficking organization.

52 If you speak another language, offer to interpret for rescued victims.

53 Organize an anti-trafficking film festival. Donate part of the proceeds to a local anti-trafficking group.

54 Learn how traffickers target children. Read the U.S. Department of Education's fact sheet: www2.ed.gov/about/offices/list/osdfs/factsheet.pdf

55 Buy gifts made by girls rescued from trafficking, such as jewelry marketed by The Butterfly Project. www.butterflyprojectjewelry.org

31 facts about trafficked children

1. "At least 100,000 U.S. children (under the age of eighteen) are prostituted in the U.S. each year." (Source: National Center for Missing and Exploited Children)

2. "Thirteen years old is the average age a child enters prostitution." (Source: U.S. Department of Justice)

3. "The average age of entry into pornography and prostitution in the U.S. is twelve." (Source: Shared Hope International, *The National Report on Domestic Minor Sex Trafficking: America's Prostituted Children*)

4. "An estimated 2.8 million kids live on the streets in the U.S." (Source: Shared Hope International, *The National Report on Domestic Minor Sex Trafficking: America's Prostituted Children*)

5. "Within forty-eight hours of leaving home, one-third of runaways are lured into prostitution." (Source: Shared Hope International, *The National Report on Domestic Minor Sex Trafficking: America's Prostituted Children*)

6. "Minors can be sold ten to fifteen times a night, six nights a week." (Source: Shared Hope International, *The National Report on Domestic Minor Sex Trafficking: America's Prostituted Children*)

7. "Each year in the United States, at least 100,000 children are at risk for being exploited in the commercial sex industry." (Source: Shared Hope International)

8. "Sixty-five percent of the johns [buyers] that go on the Internet are more responsive if the ads have age descriptors like 'young' or 'barely legal' attached to them." (Source: Kaffie McCullough,

A Future Not a Past/Juvenile Justice Fund, quoted in Shared Hope International, *The National Report on Domestic Minor Sex Trafficking: America's Prostituted Children*)

9 "Children exploited through prostitution report they typically are given a quota by their trafficker/pimp of ten to fifteen buyers per night, though some service providers report girls having been sold to as many as forty-five buyers in a night at peak demand times, such as during a sports event or convention." (Source: Shared Hope International, *The National Report on Domestic Minor Sex Trafficking: America's Prostituted Children*)

10 "Utilizing a conservative estimate, a DMST [domestic minor sex trafficking victim] who is rented for sex acts with five different men per night, for five nights per week, for an average of five years, would be raped by 6,000 buyers during the course of her victimization." (Source: Shared Hope International, *The National Report on Domestic Minor Sex Trafficking: America's Prostituted Children*)

11 "Most buyers of sexual services from minors receive little or no punishment, while many of the child victims are arrested and charged with the crime committed against them." (Source: Shared Hope International, *The National Report on Domestic Minor Sex Trafficking: America's Prostituted Children*)

12 "Some common facilitators in the crime of domestic minor sex trafficking include taxi drivers, hotel workers, and owners of adult sexual entertainment venues. Taxi drivers in Las Vegas receive commissions for bringing buyers to illegal suburban house brothels." (Sources: Demand, Shared Hope International: July 2007; Kennedy and Pucci, Domestic Minor Sex Trafficking Assessment Report, Las Vegas, Nevada)

13   "The average age that a pimp recruits a girl into prostitution is twelve to fourteen years old. They know how to target the girls who are the most vulnerable. Her greatest vulnerability is her age." (Source: Linda Smith, founder and president, Shared Hope International)

14   "Traffickers as well as buyers strategically prey upon runaway children because of their mental, physical, and financial vulnerability." (Source: Shared Hope International, *The National Report on Domestic Minor Sex Trafficking: America's Prostituted Children*)

15   "An estimate 1.68 million children run away each year in the U.S." (Source: National Incidence Studies of Missing, Abducted, Runaway, and Thrownaway Children)

16   "Seventy percent of domestic minor sex trafficking victims in the U.S. have experienced physical or sexual abuse in their homes." (Source: Shared Hope International, *The National Report on Domestic Minor Sex Trafficking: America's Prostituted Children*)

17   "One out of every five pornographic images is of a child. Fifty-five percent of child pornography comes from the U.S." (Source: Shared Hope International)

18   "The sale of child pornography in the U.S. has become more than a $3 billion annual industry." (Source: Shared Hope International)

19   "Eighty-three percent of buyers said jail time and seventy-nine percent said a letter sent to their family would be a deterrent to purchasing sex with a minor." (Source: *Deconstructing the Demand for Prostitution*, Chicago Alliance Against Sexual Exploitation)

20   "Traffickers sell underage girls for $400 an hour or more." (Source: *Demand* by Shared Hope International)

21 "Despite laws abolishing hereditary slavery in many countries, girls born into slavery are still forced to marry men who buy them as 'fifth wives' and subsequently subject them to forced labor and sexual servitude." (Source: 2012 Trafficking in Persons Report)

22 "In some countries children from ages four to fourteen are subjected to forced labor working as many as eighteen hours a day to weave rugs destined for export markets in the U.S. and Europe." (Source: 2012 Trafficking in Persons Report)

23 "The stigma and marginalization of children with disabilities creates a particular vulnerability. For example, parents who see no hope of jobs or marriage for their disabled children may place them in exploitative situations with the intent of shedding a 'burden' or seeking income." (Source: 2012 Trafficking in Persons Report)

24 "Girls with disabilities are often assumed to be virgins and thus targeted for forced sex, including by HIV-positive individuals who believe that having sex with a virgin will cure them." (Source: Global HIV/AIDS survey, World Bank and Yale University)

25 "Where schools fail to accommodate students with disabilities, high drop-out rates leave them on the streets and at much higher risk of being trafficked in forced begging or other activities." (Source: 2012 Trafficking in Persons Report)

26 "Following the earthquake in Haiti and the tsunami in Asia, thousands of children were separated from their parents. Traffickers immediately began preying upon vulnerable at-risk children." (Source: Born2Fly Project)

27 "The current accepted estimate of the number of persons (adults and children) enslaved around the world is 20.9 million." (Source: International Labor Organization)

28 "Fifty-five percent of victims of forced labor victims are women and girls. Ninety-eight percent of victims of sex trafficking are women and girls." (Source: International Labor Organization)

29 "If there were no demand for commercial sex, sex trafficking would not exist in the form it does today...Too often, trafficking victims are wrongly discounted as 'consenting' adults." (Source: 2013 Trafficking in Persons Report)

30 "Many of Haiti's trafficking cases are the estimated 150,000–500,000 children in forced domestic service." (Source: 2013 Trafficking in Persons Report)

31 "In some African and Latin American countries, traditional witchcraft plays a role in facilitating modern slavery. *Juju* oaths—once used to protect individuals about to undertake a new challenge or journey—are now abused by traffickers to tie victims to silence and obedience." (Source: 2013 Trafficking in Persons Report)

Resources

Born2Fly resources

All Born2Fly anti-trafficking materials—curriculums, radio scripts, and more—are available for free download. Fill out a short application form at www.born2fly.org. Once we approve your application, we'll send you a password to download the materials without charge. We add new materials and translations all the time; once you're approved you can check back whenever you like and download new materials. We'll also email you regular updates with more information and ideas to help you teach B2F to children, teens, and young adults.

Born to Fly curriculum

Six-session curriculum with separate, age-appropriate tracks for young children and teenagers. Available digitally as a pdf in English, Spanish, Russian, simplified Chinese (mainland), Thai, Hindi, Bisayan (Philippines), Nepali, Indonesian, and other languages.

Born to Fly wordless book

Companion book to curriculum; wordless so that children anywhere in the world can "read" it. Eighty pages with 500 illustrations by artist Leah Wiedemer. Available digitally as a pdf.

Soaring Higher curriculum

Companion to regular *Born to Fly* curriculum with additional lesson material for Christian schools. Available digitally as a pdf in English, Spanish, Russian, simplified Chinese (mainland), Thai, Hindi, Bisayan (Philippines), Nepali, Indonesian, and other languages

Dream Big Campaign curriculum

Curriculum specifically for teens and young adults. Available digitally as a pdf.

Dream Big With God curriculum

Companion to *Dream Big Campaign* curriculum with additional lesson material for Christian schools. Available digitally as a pdf.

Born to Fly radio

Scripts and music for ten-episode dramatized radio program for children based on the *Born to Fly* storyline to teach trafficking awareness. Available digitally as pdf and mp3 files.

If you'd like to translate any of these resources into another language, please write for more information: info@born2fly.org.

Other resources

Awareness materials

Human trafficking indicators card. www.dhs.gov/xlibrary/assets/ht_ice_tipcard.pdf

Coming to the U.S. to work or study? U.S. government pamphlet on how to protect yourself, your rights, etc., with a section on how to stay safe from human trafficking. www.travel.state.gov/pdf/Pamphlet-Order.pdf

Multilingual phrasebook for victim identification: A phrasebook with twelve questions to help determine if someone is a victim of human trafficking. Translated into forty-seven languages. Made available by Free for Life and Doctors at War. www.freeforlifeintl.org/multilingual-phrase-book

Global anti-trafficking hotlines: Numbers and organizations where you can report trafficking in dozens of countries from Albania to Zimbabwe. www.state.gov/j/tip/rls/other/2011/168859.htm

Information and fact sheets

For information on pending legislation in the U.S. www.polarisproject.org/what-we-do/policy-advocacy/national-policy/all-pending-legislation

Tools for service providers, health care professionals, law enforcement, and others. www.polarisproject.org/resources/tools-for-service-providers-and-law-enforcement

General info and resources from Polaris Project. www.polarisproject.org/resources/resources-by-topic/human-trafficking

Trafficking in Persons Report from U.S. Department of State updated each June. www.state.gov/j/tip/rls/tiprpt/2013/index.htm

AUDACIOUS

Resources for law enforcement from U.S. Department of Homeland Security. www.dhs.gov/law-enforcement-resources

Services available to victims of human trafficking in the U.S. from U.S. Department of Health and Human Services. www.acf.hhs.gov/sites/default/files/orr/traffickingservices_0.pdf

Blue campaign resource catalog from U.S. Department of Homeland Security's campaign against human trafficking. www.dhs.gov/blue-campaign-resource-catalog

Goods produced by child labor or forced labor from U.S. Department of Labor. www.dol.gov/ilab/programs/ocft/PDF/2009TVPRA.pdf

Training

Human trafficking awareness training from U.S. Department of Homeland Security. www.dhs.gov/xlibrary/training/dhs_awareness_training_fy12/hta01/module.htm?refresh=1&

Training resources for law enforcement. www.dhs.gov/anti-human-trafficking-resources-law-enforcement

Reports

Shared Hope International, *The National Report on Domestic Minor Sex Trafficking: America's Prostituted Children.* www.sharedhope.org

State-by-state reporting of trafficking. Keep in mind that just because a state has a high number of reported instances doesn't mean it has a higher rate of trafficking than elsewhere; it just means there is more reporting. www.polarisproject.org/state-map

Videos

Backstory: MTV's Interactive Anti-Slavery Campaign Interactive videos that show youth how poor choices can lead to being trafficked. www.thebackstory.mtv.com

Freedom Acts: Forced Labor Adam's story of how he was exploited for forced labor in Northern Ireland. www.youtube.com/watch?v=g-LHSBC2u3M

Freedom Acts: Grooming Alisha's story of how she was groomed for sexual exploitation as a teenager in Northern Ireland. www.youtube.com/watch?v=ISKgm0-xX70

Freedom Acts: Sexual Exploitation Anna's story of how she was tricked and forced into sexual exploitation in Northern Ireland. www.youtube.com/watch?v=DKzah7Rg0ks

Freedom Acts: The Conclusion The end of Adam, Alisha, and Anna's stories along with more information. www.youtube.com/watch?v=txSkdQQC92c

Journey to Freedom True stories of two men sold into slavery more than 150 years apart, and the abolitionists who fight to free slaves. http://freedomcenter.org/journey-to-freedom/

Warning to Young Women in China Video in Mandarin Chinese with English subtitles; a good warning to young women everywhere, not just in China. www.youtube.com/watch?feature=player_embedded&v=p1EzhrO2Fwl

Films

China's Stolen Children www.hbo.com/documentaries/chinas-stolen-children

Nefarious: Merchant of Souls www.nefariousdocumentary.com

Not Today www.nottodaythemovie.com

Apps

Kid Rescue. In Colombia when someone sees a child working illegally they can take a picture with their phone and log the location, which the app sends to the country's child welfare agency. In apps, search "Kid Rescue."

For more reading

A Crime So Monstrous: Face-to-Face with Modern Day Slavery, by E. Benjamin Skinner

Escaping the Devil's Bedroom, by Dawn Herzog Jewell

Girls Like Us: Fighting for a World Where Girls are Not for Sale, an Activist Finds Her Calling and Heals Herself, by Rachel Lloyd

God in a Brothel: An Undercover Journey into Sex Trafficking and Rescue, by Daniel Walker

Good News About Injustice: A Witness of Courage in a Hurting World, by Gary Haugen

In Our Backyard: A Christian Perspective on Human Trafficking in the United States, by Nita Belles

Just Courage: God's Great Expedition for the Restless Christian, by Gary Haugen

Justice Wrapped in Mercy, by Sharon Gonzales

Land of the Free: A Prayer Guide to End Human Trafficking in America, by Nicholas Canuso

Not For Sale: The Return of the Global Slave Trade, by David Batstone

Priceless, by Tom Davis

Renting Lacy: A Story of America's Prostituted Children, by Linda Smith with Cindy Coloma

The Road of Lost Innocence: The True Story of a Cambodian Heroine, by Somaly Mam

Slave Hunter: One Man's Global Quest to Free Victims of Human Trafficking, by Aaron Cohen

Slavery Today: A Groundwork Guide, by Kevin Bales and Becky Cornell

Terrify No More: Young Girls Held Captive and the Daring Undercover Operation to Win Their Freedom, by Gary Haugen

The Slave Across the Street: The True Story of How an American Teen Survived the World of Human Trafficking, by Teresa L. Flores with PeggySue Wells

The Slave Next Door: Human Trafficking and Slavery in America Today, by Kevin Bales and Ron Soodalter

Unveiled, by Vinita Shaw

Contact information

 The Born2Fly Project
P.O. Box 952949
Lake Mary, Florida 32795, U.S.A.

 www.born2fly.org

 www.dianascimone.com

 info@born2fly.org

 @DianaScimone

 www.causes.com/born2fly

169

AUDACIOUS

Made in the USA
San Bernardino, CA
08 January 2016